THE LOOKOUT

❖

Scale Colour

Scale colour

The effect of light on colour is mentioned in two articles in this issue. With this in mind, it is worth discussing scale colour in more detail. In practically every reference I have read about the painting of ship models the author writes about the true, full-size colours used on the original ship and how best to match these on the model. In some cases author-model makers have even advocated using the same paint as the original, thereby ensuring what they believe is 100 per cent accuracy. However, when scaling down an original to 1/48, 1/100, or whatever scale is chosen, we rarely if ever consider scaling down the colour.

Marine artists 'scale' colours to suit both the scale of the painting and the light being depicted (which can and does have a drastic effect on perceived colour). Without this scaling down of colour most representational or narrative paintings would be considered garish and unacceptable. Committed architectural, aircraft and railway model-makers frequently scale colours down to complement the scale of the model, but ship model-makers do not, even when weathering is applied.

At one exhibition an award-winning model of a Victorian period battleship was presented in full-size colours; black hull, white superstructure and cream or buff funnels. Other details were also in full-size colours. While the craftsmanship was undoubtedly excellent the over-all effect, because of the use of full-size colours, was to render the model as if nothing more than a toy. Ship-builder's models were often the worst offenders of this practice, combining full-size colours with brass and chrome-plated fittings. This may have impressed city-bound executives but it did nothing to reflect the true nature of the subject.

A study of even black-and-white photographs will reveal that a black hull will actually be a shade of grey, the shade itself being determined by distance, and prevailing light. White superstructure too will appear as shades of grey. The crucial factor is that the colours lose their intensity – their saturation – by the distance they are from the observer. This is no different from a ship model. The use of a warm and very dark grey instead of black, as but one example, will still be perceived as being black. And when put alongside a comparable model, which has used 'full-size' black, the scale difference will imme-

The wooden barque *Carmen. Photographs from Michael Leek's collection.*

West German training barque *Gorch Foch*.

It might be that to take this step towards scale colour ship model makers might be fearful of ruining months if not years of hard work. This is understandable so the answer therefore is to do a series of comparative tests before applying to a model. I believe the reaction will be positively received and, when applied, will enhance any ship model.

The two photographs show a common theme, yet are separated in time by at least forty years; the need for steam to assist sail in the confined waters of a port or harbour. The first shows the Hamburg-registered wooden barque *Carmen* being towed out to sea in 1918, while the second shows the West German Navy training barque *Gorch Foch* in the early 1960s. They are reproduced here primarily for their visual appeal, but also as possible sources of inspiration for dioramas and to demonstrate how full-size colours are reduced to shades of grey, including the white hull of the *Gorch Foch*. ❑

diately become apparent. In very basic terms, the larger the scale of the model (1/48 and larger) the closer to 'full-size' black that can be used . The smaller the scale the more diluted the 'full-size' colour needs to be. Unintentional examples can be seen in museums where the colours on models of 150 or more years old have faded because of ultra violet light, yet we still describe the colours as if full size.

The Tasmanian Barque *Nautilus*, 1872–1891

(Part 1)

by John Laing

Early in 1873, my great-great uncle John Cox signed on as a seaman on the Tasmanian barque *Nautilus* in order to return to England to visit his father's family.

Unfortunately he never lived to see his English relatives as he fell from the main topsail yardarm during a storm off the Cape of Good Hope and was lost overboard. His death was eventually reported in the Tasmanian newspapers after receipt of a letter from Cape Town setting out the circumstances of the accident.

Having almost completed my first plank-on-frame model, I was looking for a new ship to model, and was attracted to the small wooden sailing ships that had been built in Tasmania in the latter part of the nineteenth century. Was the *Nautilus*, connected so tragically with a distant ancestor, one of those ships? If she was, she might be the perfect prototype for my next building task, both the type of ship I was looking for and with a family connection to make the project more personal.

Research and plans

The first job was to find the right *Nautilus*. *Nautilus* was a fairly common name for sailing ships in the 1870s, but thankfully the newspaper reports of John Cox's death

The painting of *Nautilus*.

Courtesy of the National Maritime Museum, Tasmania.

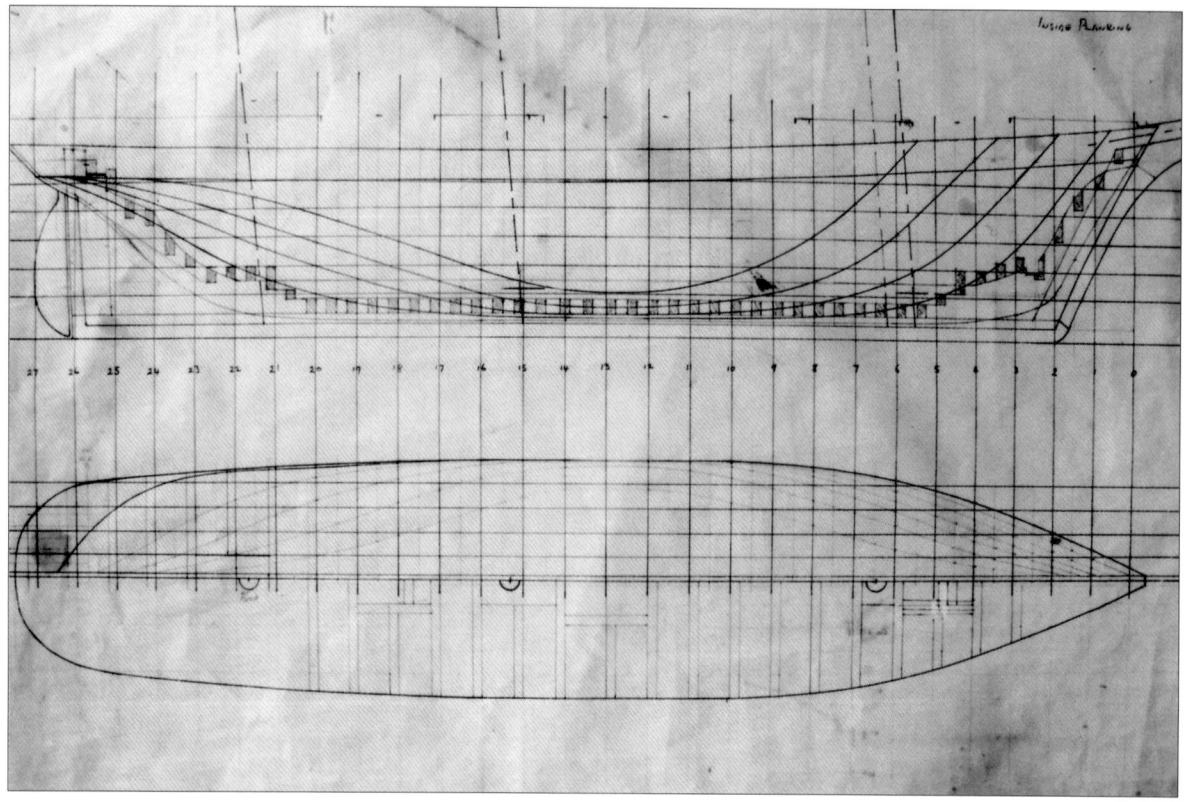

Lines plan.

included the name of the ship's Master – Captain Hopkins – and noted that *Nautilus* was a barque. That narrowed the field a bit, and with the help of several books on the early maritime history of Tasmania, I soon narrowed the field down to a small wooden barque built in Hobart by Mackey's in 1872.

Next I contacted the Maritime Museum of Tasmania to confirm that my suppositions were correct and I was not letting myself be led astray by wishful thinking. The very helpful folk in Hobart confirmed that I had indeed found the right ship. *Nautilus* was built by the firm of J & D Mackey at their Battery Point yard to the order of Mr Henry Hopkins, a prominent Tasmanian businessman. Hopkins had her built as a cargo-carrying yacht with the intention of taking her for a world cruise, with the cargo carried helping to pay the expenses. She was 129

feet overall length with a beam of 26 feet and a depth of 14 feet. She was built from local timbers, with her keel, keelson and stringers all being made from single lengths of timber each 112 feet long.

Hopkins sailed to Europe with a cargo of wheat in January 1873 (the voyage that proved so unfortunate for John Cox), and did not return to Hobart until late December (it was, after all, a pleasure cruise), but this was the only voyage on which *Nautilus* was employed as a yacht. Hopkins put her on a regular run to China and she became Tasmania's only regular 'tea clipper'.

On Hopkins' death in 1875 she was sold to another Tasmanian businessman, Hugh Armstrong, who employed her in the colonial trade until he sold her to the Colonial Sugar Refining Company in 1887. She was used by that company for trading to the South Pacific and the end came in August 1891, when she

was completely burnt out at Noumea, New Caledonia.

So much for the very interesting history of the *Nautilus*, but was there enough available information to enable me to build a model? There are (one might almost say, 'naturally') no surviving plans for the *Nautilus*. The Maritime Museum of Tasmania has a fine oil painting of her – thought to have been painted when she was new – and there is also an unrigged model in the same museum which shows her on the slips ready for launching; even down to the bottle of champagne at the bow. There is a surviving plan of one of Mackey's ships similar to the *Nautilus*, and I also found a postcard of her (taken from another painting) in the State Library of Victoria.

A friend visiting Tasmania was able to photograph the model for me, including an excellent profile view and a full bow view, together with deck details. The (again) helpful folk at the museum very kindly sketched for me the shape of the bow and stern at deck level. I also obtained copies of the two known paintings.

Armed with all of the above information I was able to draw an accurate outboard profile in both plan and elevation; but how to turn that into a set of hull lines? I could see the shape of the hull plainly from the photographs of the model, but a shape only visualised is hardly enough to use to draft a set of frames for a plank-on-frame model. I went back to traditional methods and made a half model out of western red cedar built up in seven narrow horizontal lifts to the exact dimensions of the proposed model, and held together with soluble glue. Once the profiles were carved in the block it was simply a matter of carving down the hull until the half model matched the shape I could see on the photographs of the Tasmanian model. The half model was then taken apart and the lifts used as waterlines to draw up the hull lines.

Instead of drawing a fully detailed plan, I drew only the hull lines and had a photographer friend make me an enlargement of one of the paintings so that I could take dimensions directly from that. The photographic enlargement turned out to be not quite the correct size, but it was a simple matter to use a small conversion factor on all dimensions taken off.

The model

The model was built at a scale of 1:96 (⅛in = 1ft), giving a hull length of about 16in (40.6cm). This gave a nice finished size to the model for fitting into the average home without problems, and I find it a nice scale to work with; most detail can be shown and it is a bit of a challenge as well.

The hull. The framing was made of pine taken from a 100-year-old table top; milled and sanded to ⅛in thick. The keel, stem and sternpost were hand cut to shape and joined at the correct angles, with weights holding them completely flat when they had been glued. Once the glue was fully cured the joints were dowelled to give them additional strength, and the fore and aft deadwoods were built up of small offcuts; glued and dowelled in place. The positions of the frames were then marked on the keel and deadwoods with an ⅛in space between each frame, and the rabbet was marked out and cut. Care was taken to ensure that the rabbet was correctly cut across the deadwoods; any error in doing this will mean that the planking will not lie properly across these critical areas.

The completed backbone was placed on the building board and set up between right-angle brackets fore and aft and with chocks on either

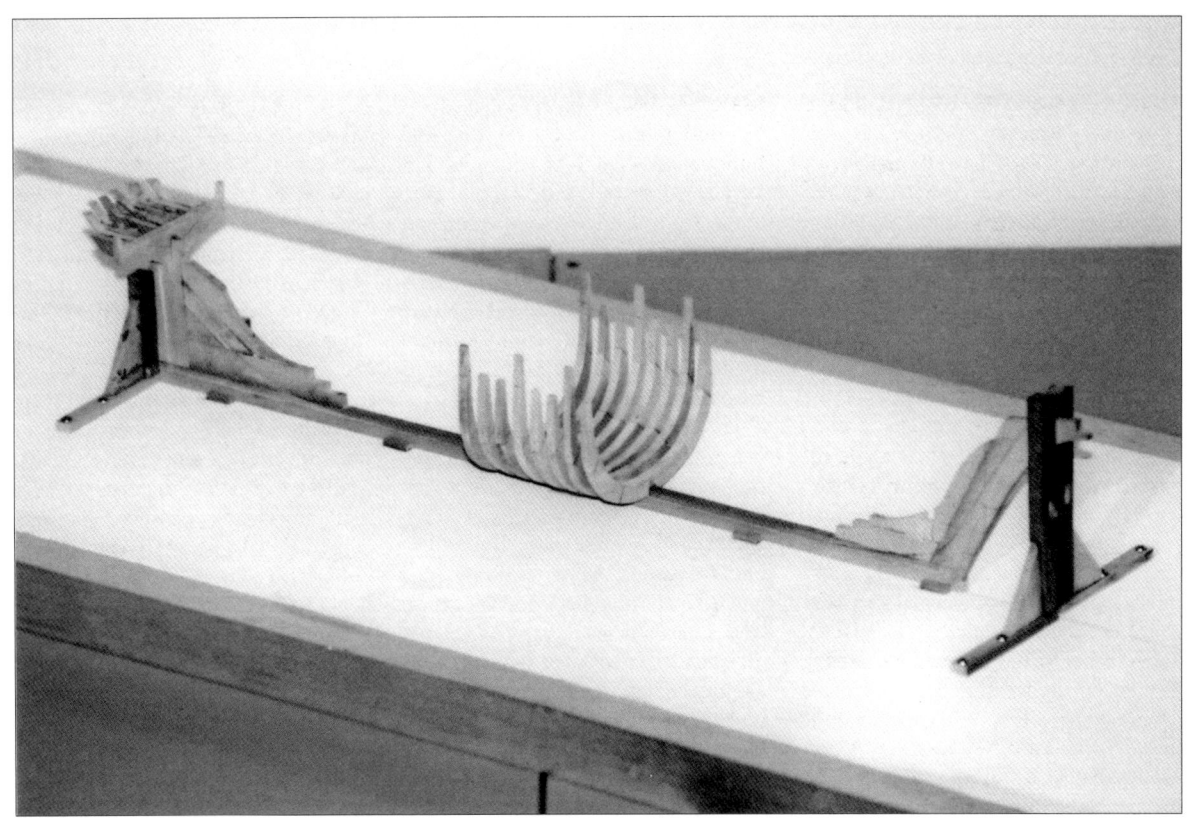

Stem, keel and sternpost assembly with first group of midship frames fitted.

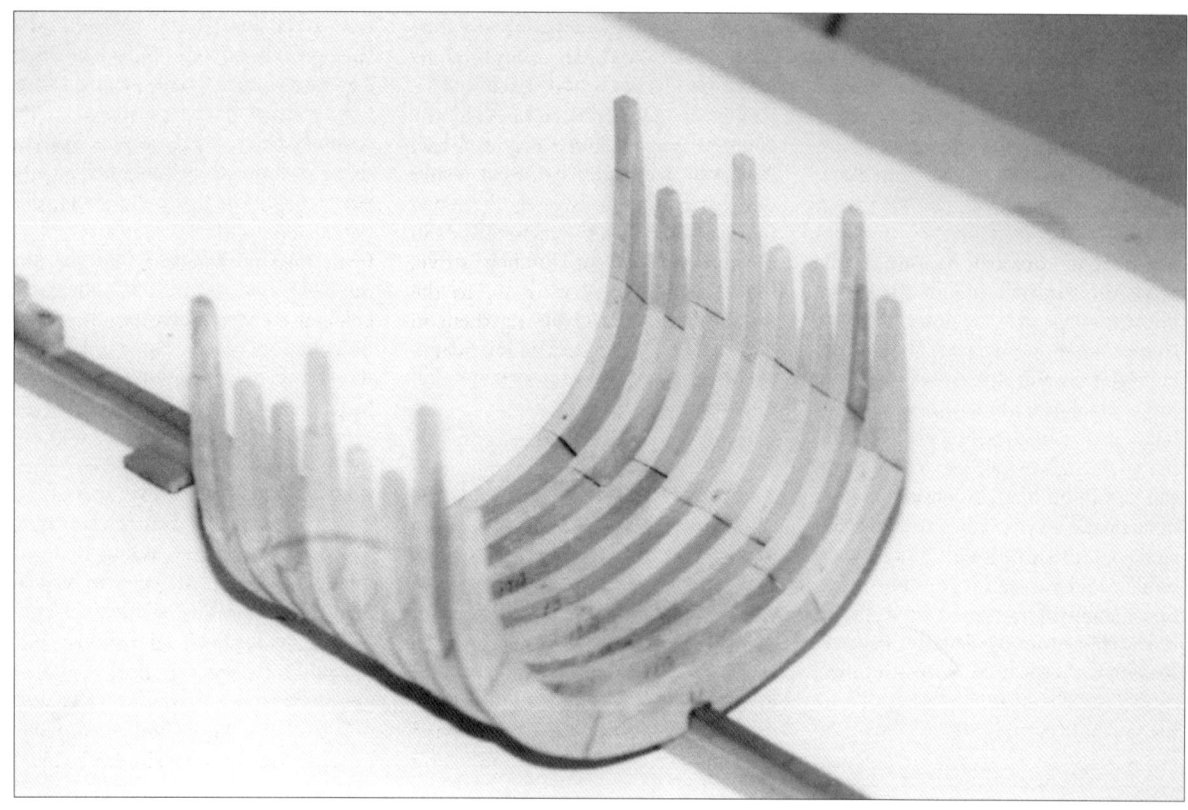

Close-up detail of group of midship frames.

side of the keel. The building board was a piece of particle board strengthened with metal angles to ensure it remained completely flat. The model remained on this building board until all the frames were in place, and the keelson, stringers, deck shelves and rubbing strakes had been fitted, to ensure that it could not warp or twist during these early stages of construction.

Each frame was made up of several short sections of timber to ensure that the grain followed the curve of the frame. Most frames consisted of seven separate sections. Each frame was drawn out on tracing paper and the individual sections were then glued to the paper and to each other. They were held completely flat by weights while the glue dried; they were then drilled and fitted with dowels. When they were quite dry, the frames were cut to shape, bevelled inside and outside, and the mortice for the keel cut.

The bulwark stanchions were included as an integral part of the frames, there being a stanchion at every third frame in the general run of the hull, and at every frame in way of the masts. It was thought that this method of construction would result in a much stronger structure at the upper deck, rather than following full-size practice of fitting the stanchions separately.

The aftermost frame was made first as a solid unit and fitted on the fore end of the stern frame. The framing of the counter was then built up using this frame as a support. Once the counter framing was in place a framing jig, cut out of thin MDF board, was made to rest on the aftermost frame and the inboard side of the stem at main deck level. At the position of each frame a notch was cut in the jig so that the frames had positive support at the upper ends while framing was in progress. Many people use an exter-

nal jig for framing, and this certainly makes the inside of the hull far more accessible for framing, but the internal jig has the advantage on not requiring accurate vertical alignment of the keel assembly and the jig, and also means that the model can be lifted off the building board at any time without having to worry about the jig alignment.

When all the frames had been constructed and glued in place on the keel, the keelson was cut out and laid on top of the frames, where it was glued and dowelled to each frame, with the dowels being long enough to penetrate through to the keel. Thin lengths of pine were then bent into place as bilge stringers on each side and glued and dowelled to each frame. This gave the framing a fair degree of rigidity, although the frames were still vulnerable at their upper ends as they were so far totally unsupported there.

As the height of the deck had

been marked on each frame prior to fitting, it was a simple matter to mark in the height of the beam shelf below this. It was then easy to run more thin lengths of pine along each side of the hull as the beam shelves, gluing and dowelling them to each frame. The main deck shelf was run from right forward to one frame abaft the forward end of the poop, and the forecastle and poop shelves fitted in their appropriate positions.

The framework was now amazingly strong and rigid, this being helped by the number of glued and dowelled connections throughout the structure. It was now time to consider the planking, but before this was taken in hand, the rubbing strake, which could be considered to be a light wale in terms of strength, was fitted to each side of the hull. Again the material was pine and the rubbing strakes were fitted as one piece on each side as far aft as the curve of the counter to give addi-

tional strength to the structure. The rubbing strake bent easily to the form of the hull for most of its length, but the sections around the counter required steaming to shape. As the sizes required at this scale are quite small, this was easily done just by boiling them for a few minutes in a saucepan on the kitchen stove, then bending them by hand to the required shape, and drying them in the heat of a small electric fan heater. That done, they retained their new shape quite well.

Planking the hull. The next job was to plank the hull. Very careful consideration needs to be given to the size of planks and the run of the hull planking if it is to look realistic. I used a nominal plank width of ³⁄₃₂in (9in full size) with the longest planks being 3in (24ft full size). The thickness of the planks was about 1mm. The hull was divided into five even sections on each side by laying thin battens round the hull and

wiring them to the frames after measuring the distances along every fifth frame starting amidships and working fore and aft. These battens were then adjusted by eye until a fair run of planking was achieved along the entire length of the hull. This is easily done by looking at the hull from many different angles and moving the battens slightly to achieve the desired result. It is also necessary to watch the width of the planks at various points along the hull, to ensure that individual planks do not become too wide or too narrow. In the case of the *Nautilus*, with just a little adjustment of the battens, I was able to achieve full runs of planking over the entire hull without the use of stealer planks.

The material used for the hull planking was privet. Both the Chinese privet that grows in old-style hedges and the broad leaf privet produce timber very similar in char-

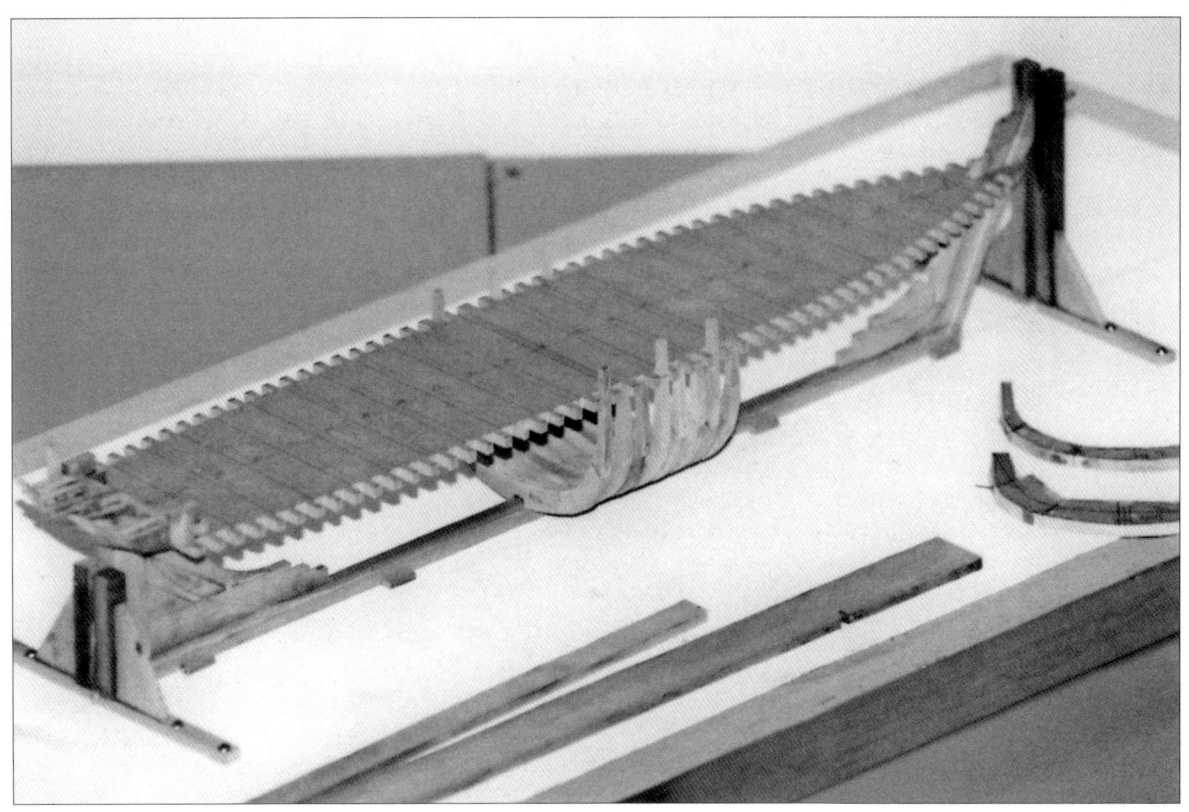

Hull framing completed.

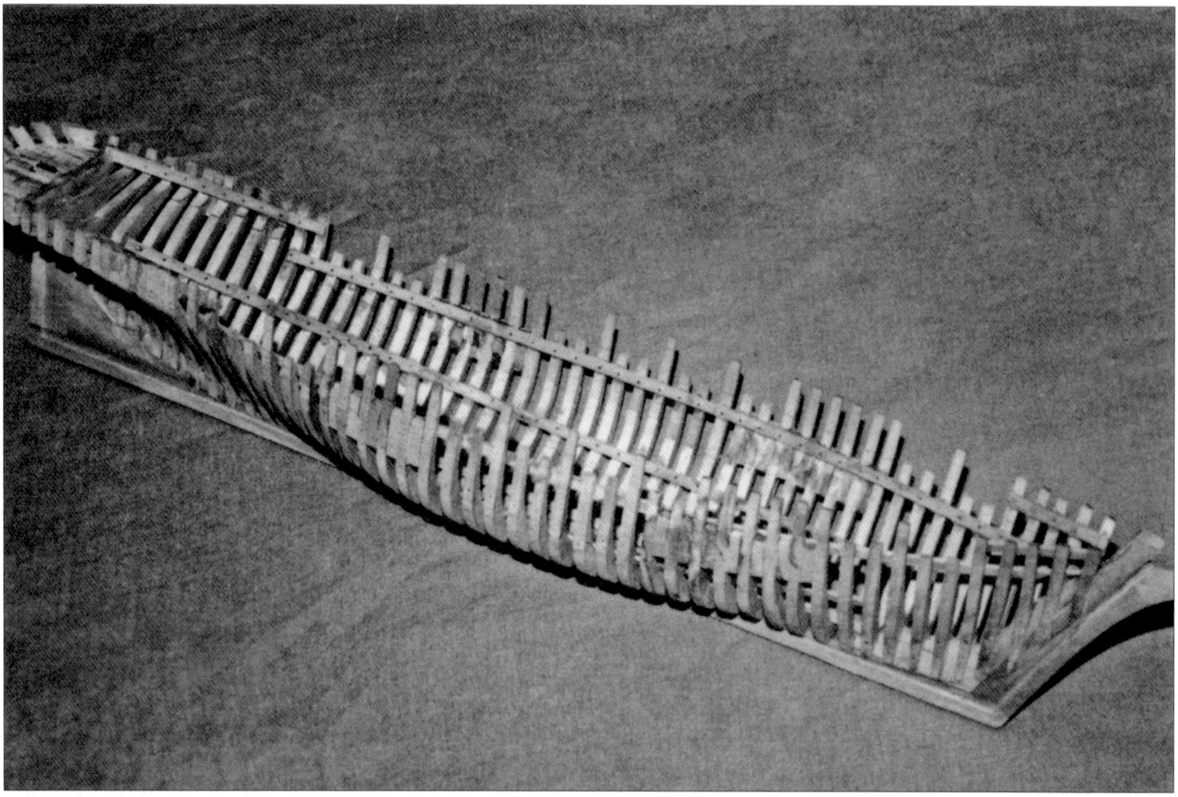

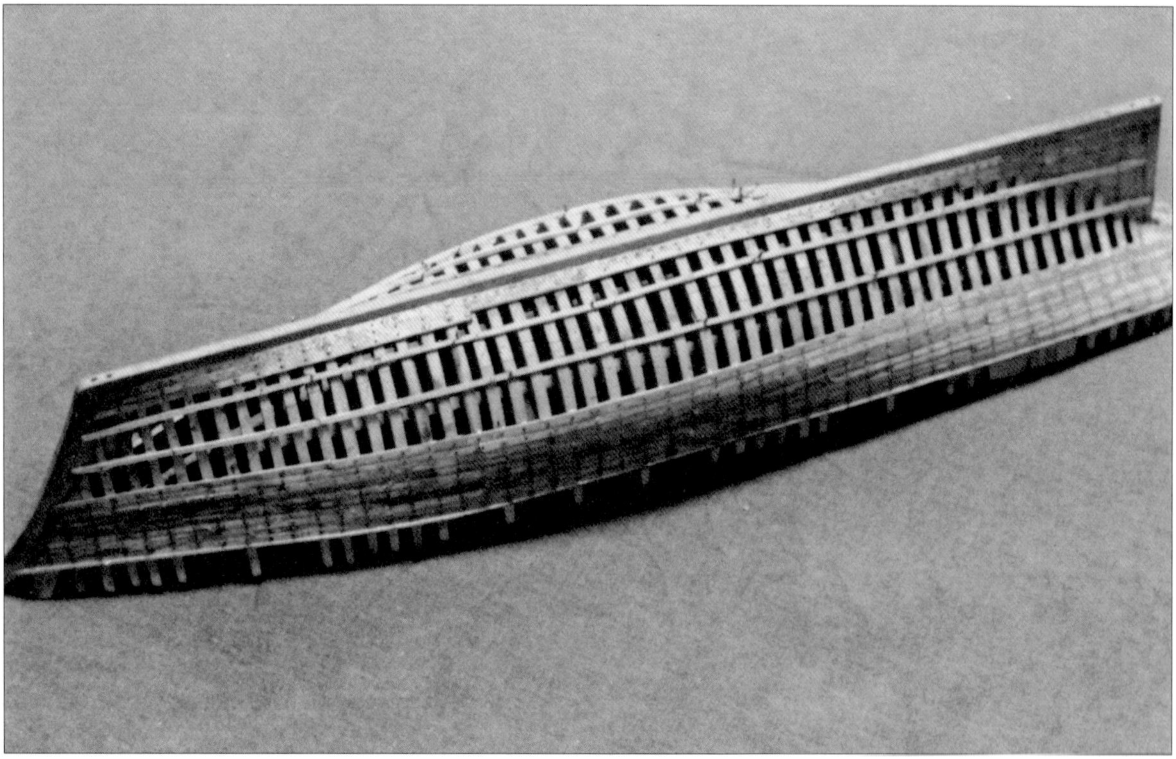

Two views of the hull ready for planking.

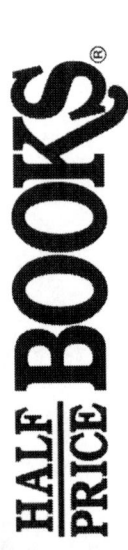

HALF PRICE BOOKS®

Half Price Books
1835 Forms Drive
Carrollton, TX 75006
OFS OrderID   37357714

SKU	ISBN/UPC	Title & Author/Artist	Shelf ID	Qty	OrderSKU
S397333963	9781844860838	Model Shipwright 144 Bowen, John	ANQ1.6	1	

ORDER# **76109051-1**
Alibris

SHIPPED STANDARD TO:
VINDY-BXC-Store
35 SW 12th Avenue, Ste 102
22315639-Y
Dania Beach FL 33004

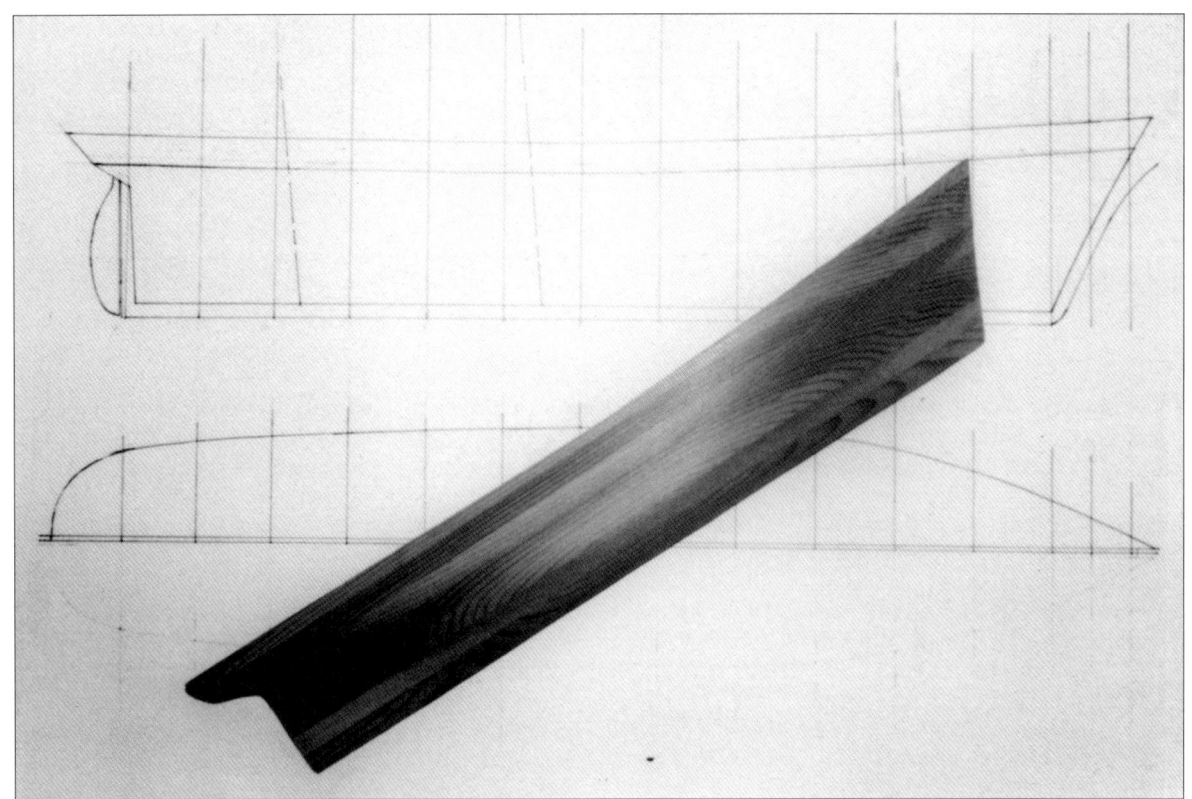

Showing the hull lying on the lines plan.

Photographs by the author.

acter to English box if allowed to grow into trees; in some parts of Australia they have become noxious weeds and quite large specimens can be found fairly easily. As they are now noxious weeds (at least where I live) there is no problem about removing them and converting them into first-class timber for model-making.

Before starting the planking, I drew out a rough planking diagram, which was simply a grid showing each frame and strake of planking as a line. On this grid I could mark in my proposed plank butts to ensure that the planking followed Lloyds' rules for the shift of butts without having to resort to over scale length planks (or to panic when I found the planks on the model getting out of sequence!).

The width of each plank was determined at each frame by the use of proportional dividers. For example, if there were three strakes of planking to fit between the completed planking and the next batten, the proportional dividers were set at position 3 and the distance from the planking to the batten was measured at each frame with the wide end of the dividers and set on the plank with the narrow end. By measuring in this way each plank was the correct width along its entire length, and any minor errors in marking or cutting a plank were taken up in the next strake of planking. This ensured that the fair run of planking was maintained throughout.

Planks were fitted alternately port and starboard to ensure that no undue stresses were set up in the hull during building. After cutting, each plank was bent to the required shape to fit the curve of the hull and test fitted for accuracy before fixing with epoxy. Privet is a very friendly timber to work with and can be gently bent and twisted to quite large curves if a little care is used. It has another advantage of retaining its new shape once bent. All the hull planks on *Nautilus* were hand bent in this manner except for those around the curve of the counter above the rubbing strake, where a little persuasion by boiling was needed.

After gluing, all planks were dowelled (tree nailed) to each frame with bamboo dowels. Bamboo is a good material to use for this purpose when small sizes are needed, as it has very good longitudinal strength down to remarkably small diameters. I was very fortunate in finding an Asian scroll picture at a garage sale that was made from fine bamboo strands of exactly the right diameter. I now have a lifetime supply.

On completion of the planking up to deck level, the entire hull was given a thorough sanding and several coats of flat polyurethane varnish to protect it before proceeding further.

(To be continued) ❏

USS *Gearing*

DD710

by John R Haynes

For some reason, the *Gearing* class of World War Two US Navy destroyer has been neglected by modellers and kit makers alike in favour of the smaller *Fletcher* class. The *Fletcher* class hull was slightly widened and used as the *Sumner* class, which in turn was lengthened to develop the ultimate World War Two *Gearing* class.

Being a modeller and not a naval historian, I will concentrate on the class leader USS *Gearing* DD710 build, and leave interested readers to investigate the naval history that resulted in their general development.

The armament carried by the USS *Gearing* comprised of 6no. 5in/38 guns in twin turrets, 3no. Quad 40mm mounts, 10no. twin 20mm Oerlikons with Mk. 14 gunsights, 2no. twin 40mm mounts and 1no. 21in quintuple torpedo tube mounting. The mainmast aerial was a SC radar with a Mk 37 main armament director atop the bridge with a MK 12 and 22 radar antenna. 5no. Mk 51 directors controlled the 40mm guns; 2 depth-charge rails with 2no. extra storage rails were mounted at the stern with 3no. depth-charge storage racks fitted each side with the associated K guns.

At 390.5 feet long overall, the model hull at my usual scale of ⅛in = 1ft (1/96) translated to 48.8in long overall, with a beam of 41.08 feet or 5.13in. Some years ago, I built a 1960s FRAM 1 (Fleet Rehabilitation and Modernisation) version for a US client, so I had already developed a grp hull that I could use with a slight modification of the hull bottom radar housing that needed to be made smaller.

Since building the FRAM version from plans provided by The Floating Drydock, USA, they now supply an e-book reference for DD710 (DD692PB-CD), that gives just about everything and more a model builder could desire. No excuse now

Port side view of bridge under construction.

Model seen from starboard quarter with most fittings loosely in place.

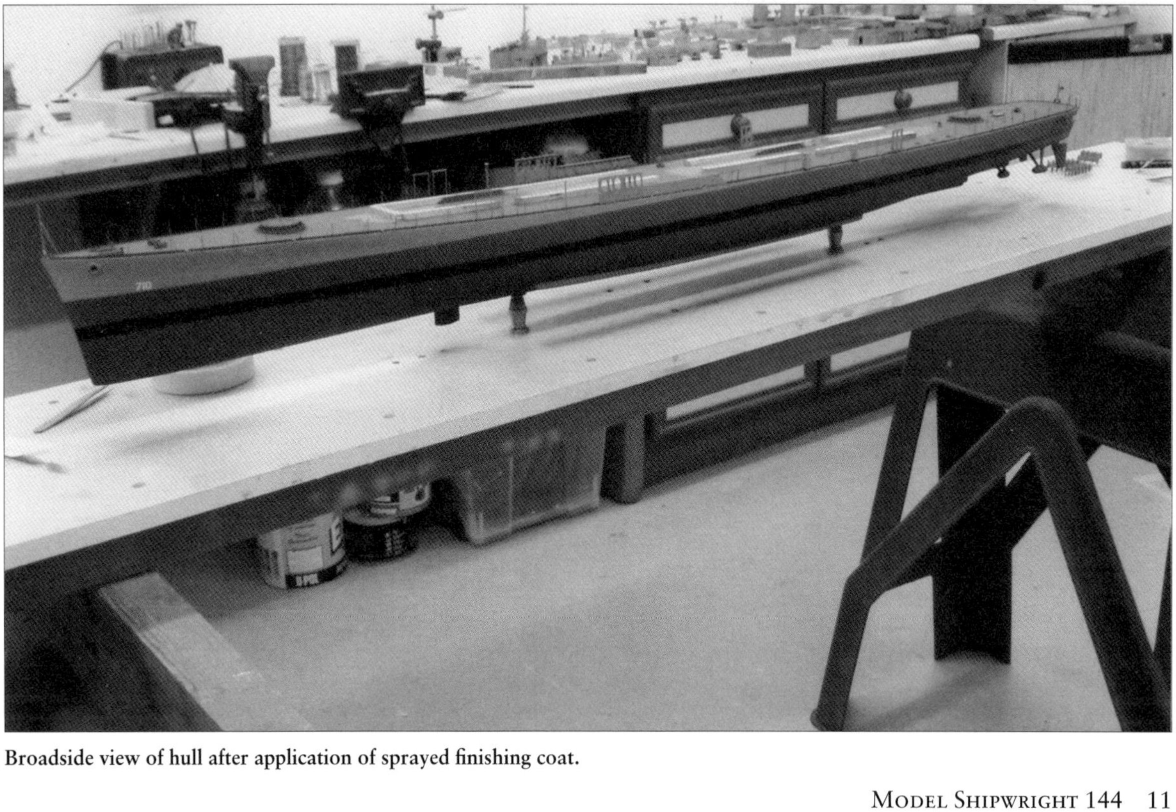

Broadside view of hull after application of sprayed finishing coat.

Overall view of port side of model.

Port depth-charge stowage racks and K guns.

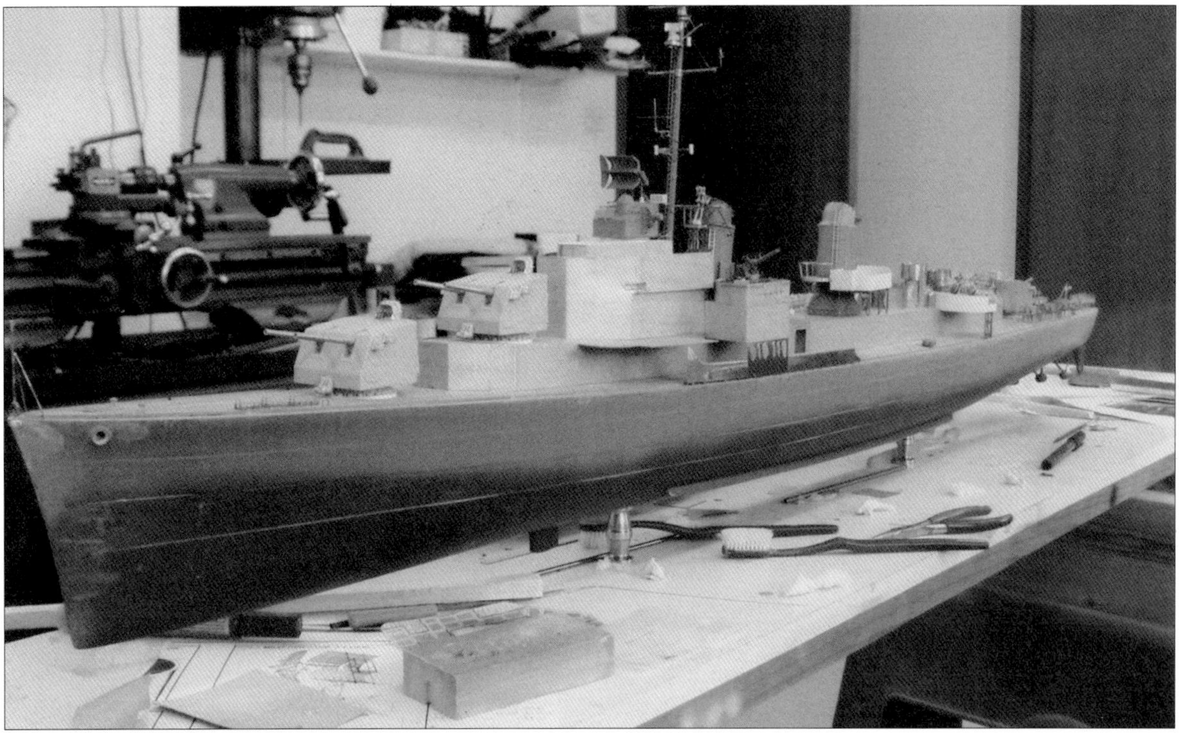

The 5in/38 DP guns are temporarily in position.

Stern details, with depth-charge rails and stowage racks, before painting.

Midships, showing quintuple torpedo tubes mounting.

Midships 40mm quad Bofors mounting with photo-etched Mk 51 director tub.

for not putting everything on that should be on. Individual drawings/photos can be printed off and used when needed. Also of use is Sumrall's book, *Sumner/Gearing Class Destroyers* and Friedman's *US Destroyers*.

On one of my visits to the United States, I was taken to Battleship Cove in Massachusetts by Mike Wall of the American Marine Model Gallery, to see the USS *Joseph P. Kennedy* DD850, a FRAM 1, and took a lot of reference photos of the smaller details.

The *Gearing* build follows my usual method of construction, namely, I build the model as a kit. During the course of construction, the model is built up and taken apart continually. This also makes the important task of finish-painting the individual parts much easier.

The hulls that I produce have an inward return built into the sheerline to maintain this line accurately. It is a useful feature that saves a lot of time even though it makes the glass-fibre more expensive.

The hull was mounted on two brass supports with bolts and the nut fixed into the bottom of the open hull. Deck beams were then inserted, cambered, and a 1/16in thick ply deck fitted. In the meantime, I am mentally constructing the model so I know where and how to 'break down' the superstructure as I build and re-assemble without leaving any visible signs. This also enables me to pick out all the new photo-etching that will be required, all the new parts to manufacture, rub-downs to initiate, paint to order, etc. Since the photo-etching takes quite a time, this task is done first. Also, I decided to

add to the decks the visible anti-slip tread rub-downs that I have not done before. I tend to favour rub-downs over decals except on my own carrier-based aircraft in my range of fittings.

On the main deck there is an upstand all round just in from the deck edge forming a spurnwater with intermittent gutters which run over the deck edge. This was formed using litho plate to make an angle and the side fixed to the deck was faired in with Milliput to eliminate the edge.

The 01 level superstructure was outlined on the deck and an eggbox structure in balsa was quickly made. This was lined on the outside with 1mm ply and finally used litho plate was also added, being taken up above the 01 deck level to form the spurnwater. I started using litho plate

Overhead view of bridge before application of sprayed finishing coat, showing the photo-etched bridge deck simulating the wood grating.

Forward funnel, showing also the base of the mast with reproducer, top of flag bags, and starboard twin Bofors platform.

some thirty years ago and have written about its use from time to time.

At this time, I needed to look at all my ship fittings now available on my site store and place the items necessary for the model in a separate box. Various new items were constructed and sent to my casters for duplication. At this point, I decide what might sell and put these items in my range.

The bridge 01 level was made similar to the 01 structure but the final litho plate was taken up beyond the 02 to form the open bridge, the deck of which was photo-etched. I always pay a lot of attention to open bridges as they attract most interest.

On the 10 thou. (0.010in) PE sheet, I included a lot of deck items such as various grilles, eyebolts, hoppers for spent 40mm ammunition, depth-charge rails and storage racks, different types of ladders, MK 51 director tubs, and most importantly, the hull side screens. The side screens have a rolled top and to achieve this,

Starboard side of bridge with pilot house and Mk 51 director, pelorus, 12in signal lamp and voice tube.

After end of bridge pilot house, showing flag bags, aerial terminals, and other detail.

Starboard side of bridge showing ventilation trunking, raft, and floatanet basket.

Close-up of front of pilot house, with a view of the fittings and photo-etched deck.

I soldered on to the flat brass half a brass tube, cut down from the round with a slitting disc. A steady hand is required to get a straight line. I tried to curve over some 5 thou. (0.005in) copper sheet but the result was not good enough and too flimsy.

On the main 01 level, there were two through-deck openings amidships. These were half-etched to achieve a rim around the square hole that left the surrounding plate at 5 thou. to match the thickness of the litho plate that met it. Other photo-etched items were pulled out of my range of fittings in various thickness of brass, namely the US Navy pattern stanchions, aerials, ladder rungs, etc.

I always leave some watertight doors open which give a better look to the model, and to this end I have now developed a small fret with six doors and frames that are available. On this model, I used the cast metal ones I had already, and these were all right but I felt photo-etched ones would be an improvement.

Other new fittings that had to be made were re-fuelling hoses, oil re-fuelling trunk, ship-to-shore cable reels, floodlamps, the funnel whistle and syren set and the funnels that were also used on the *Sumner* and *Fletcher*.

Sundry deck details, and note the floatanet basket, bottom left.

Some plastic sheet was used where I thought it was suitable but I am not a fan of this material. A sheet of brass can be bent and it will stay bent, whereas plastic needs to be held in place or it will deform. Also, the surface is more tender and any effort to correct faults or scratches will affect the look of the subsequent paint finish.

I tend to spray everything off the model, and also any hand-finishing touches needed can be easily done. After spraying the hull in Measure 22 – navy blue 5N horizontally to the deck edge at its lowest point, and the remainder haze grey 5H, I hand-painted the deck 20B blue. Having the USN purple–blue colour chart makes it very easy to get the colours correct, but I am not a believer that transferring these colours directly on to a model will give the right appearance.

Since the viewer will be seeing the model as would an aircraft, and that the weather will quickly fade the dockyard look, I tend to lighten these colours considerably. I do not mean adding white which can change the tone, but looking at the lighter colours on the chart i.e. for the deck 20B, use Humbrol 144; for hull grey 5H, use in equal quantities 127/144/130. Humbrol users will realise that this is a mixture of satin and matt. I try to do this as it gives a more forgiving finish whilst still matt in appearance; it resists finger marks and tends to take off the dead-flat look.

The reason I hand-paint the decks is that when fixing/gluing items to the painted deck during the assembly stage, the slightest scratch or glinting glue-line can be touched in successfully. It will not be a total success to touch in with a paint brush on to a sprayed finish since the paint lies on differently and it could look as if a slightly different colour was being used. Always mix up more than enough paint than the job needs and keep it in an air-tight jar.

On this particular model, before fixing the 01 assembly, I applied the anti-slip treads where indicated on the drawing and in the photographs, and I think the result is pleasing. These treads, now in my fittings range, were usually black but I decided that on a model this is too severe, so I had them made in a dark blue, which on a lighter-than-20B deck look, in my opinion, more realistic.

I find building the model is the easiest part of the work. The finishing part, spraying and painting, can enhance or detract from the final result, so care is needed to ensure the finished model is as good as possible.

(To be concluded) ❏

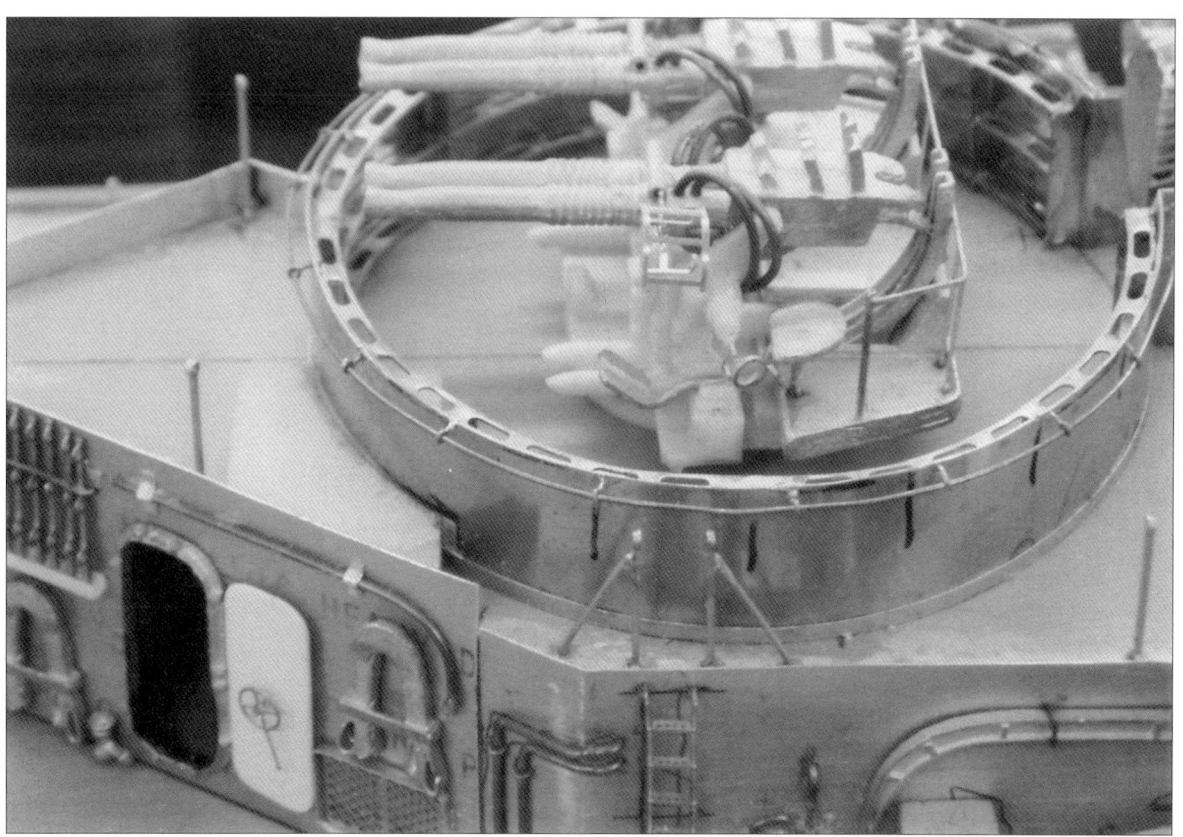

Deck level 01 with after 40mm quad Bofors mounting in tub with circular ammunition holders. *Photographs by the author.*

An 18th-Century Naval Brig

An example of a full-framed model made by the late Ewart C Freeston

by Michael Leek

The late Ewart C Freeston was a regular contributor in the early days of *Model Shipwright*. Indeed, in the very first issue, Autumn 1972, his first article was a series entitled 'Building a 17th Century Dockyard Model'. Whilst very little is known about his life, he was a prolific and highly skilled model-maker, particularly in the 1950s. He was very knowledgeable about Napoleonic prisoner-of-war models and published *Prisoner-of-War Ship Models, 1775-1825*, in 1973. As a model-maker he developed his own unique method of constructing open boats, a technique resulting in him being awarded a Model Engineer Exhibition Silver Medal in the early 1970s. Fortunately Freeston recorded some of his methods through articles for *Model Shipwright* and in his books *Model Open Boats* (1975) and *Modelling Thames Sailing Barges* (with Bernard Kent, 1972). As a long-standing member of the Society for Nautical Research Freeston was also a contributor on eighteenth-century shipbuilding for *The Mariner's Mirror*.

The beautiful, fully framed model described and illustrated here is unidentified. It was given to the Editor by Freeston's widow. Using sources such as the late David Lyon's book *The Sailing Navy List* (1993) we can only surmise that the model represents a small naval vessel, probably rigged as a brig even though there are no channels to confirm this, of a type that was used in large numbers around various naval ports and dockyards. The design (i.e. the shape) would suggest that the model further represents a vessel from the Slade Era, 1745–85.

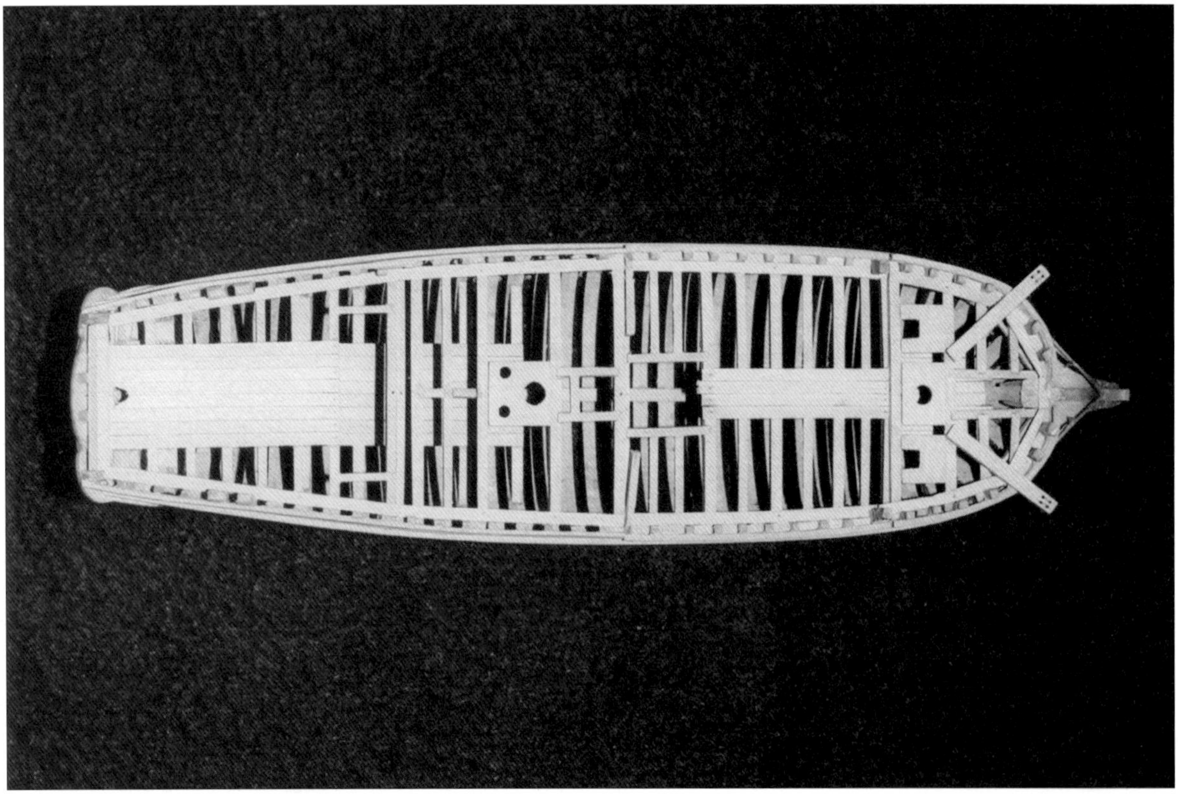

Hull seen from above showing deck layout.

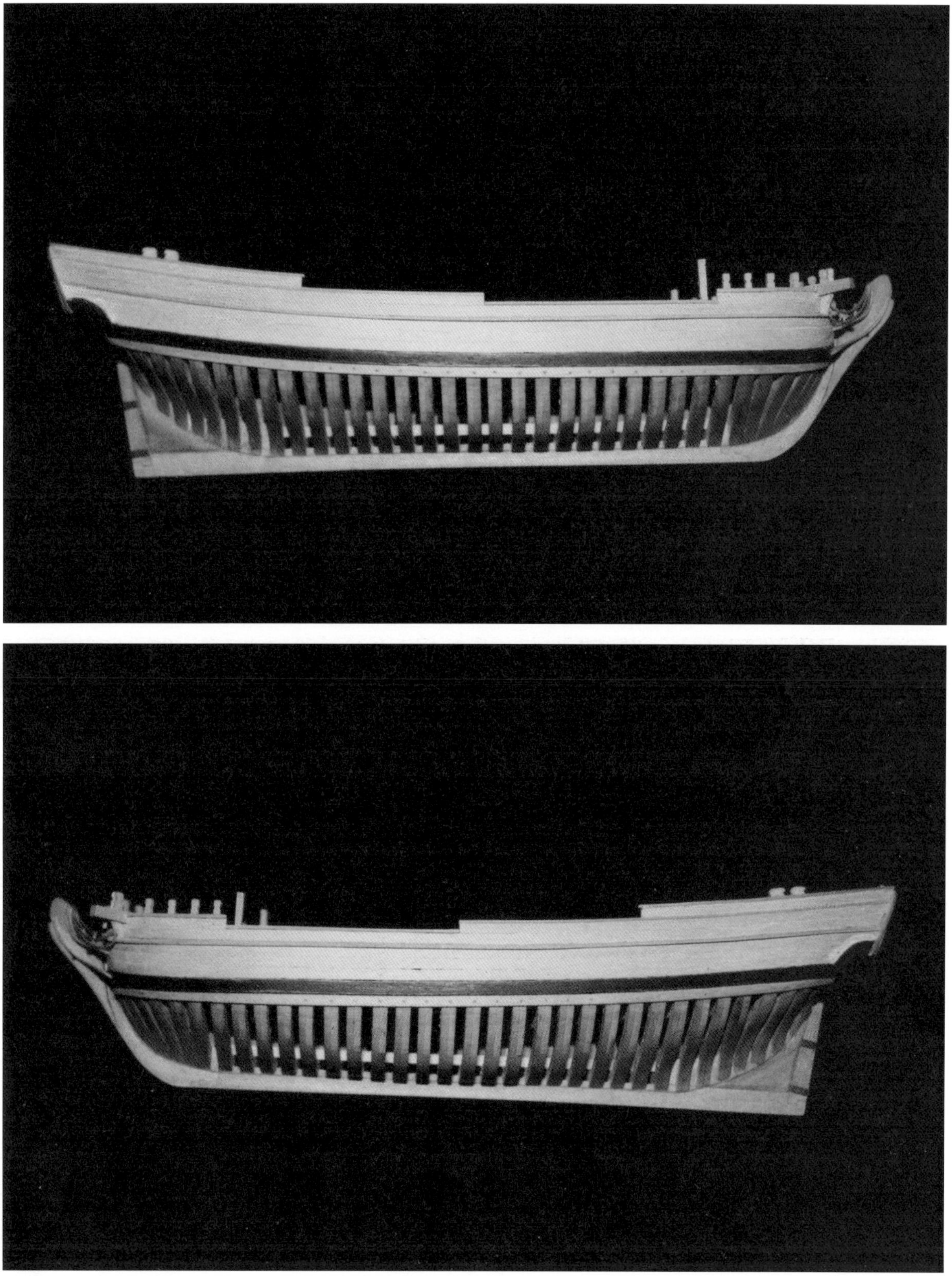

Port and starboard sides of hull.

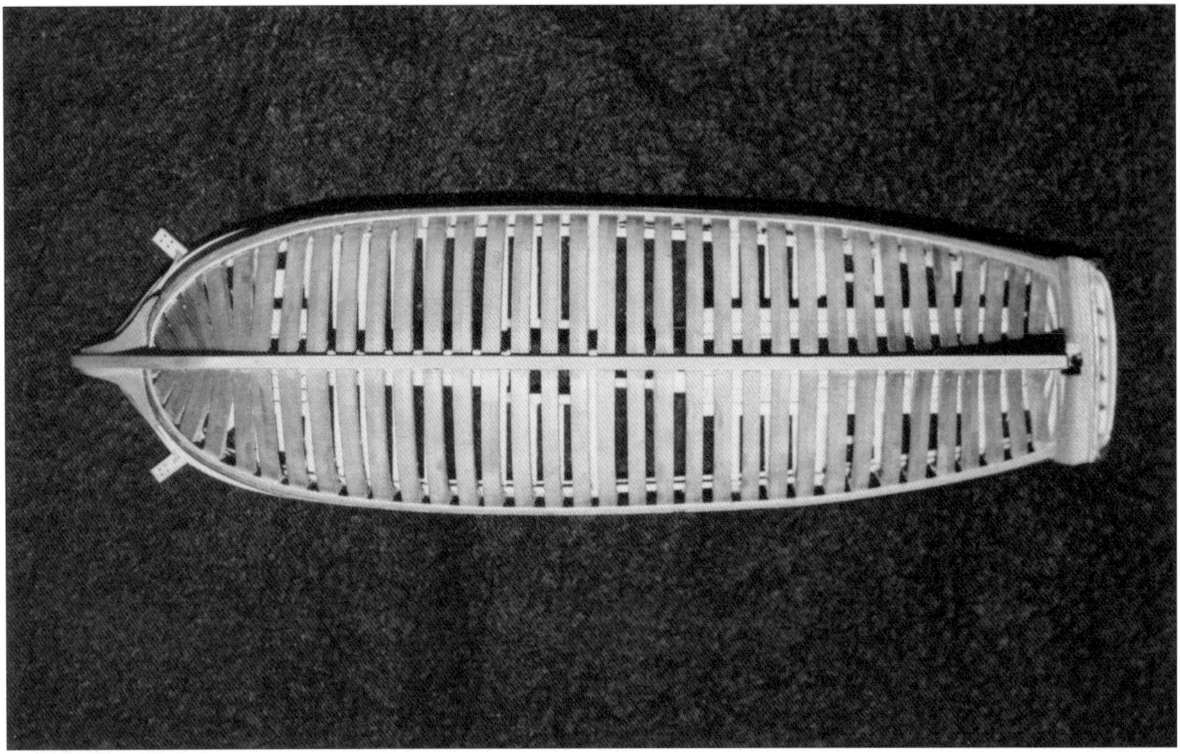

Underside of hull.

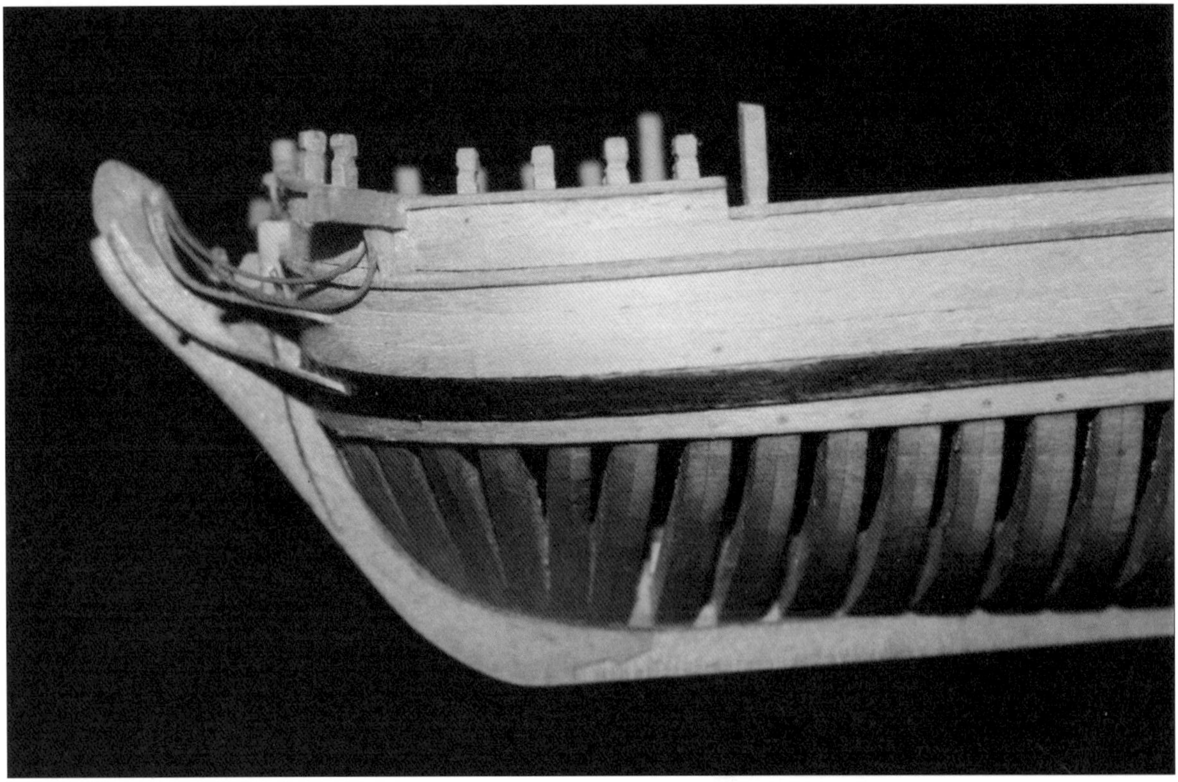

Close-up of port bow, note stem detail.

Port bow from below.

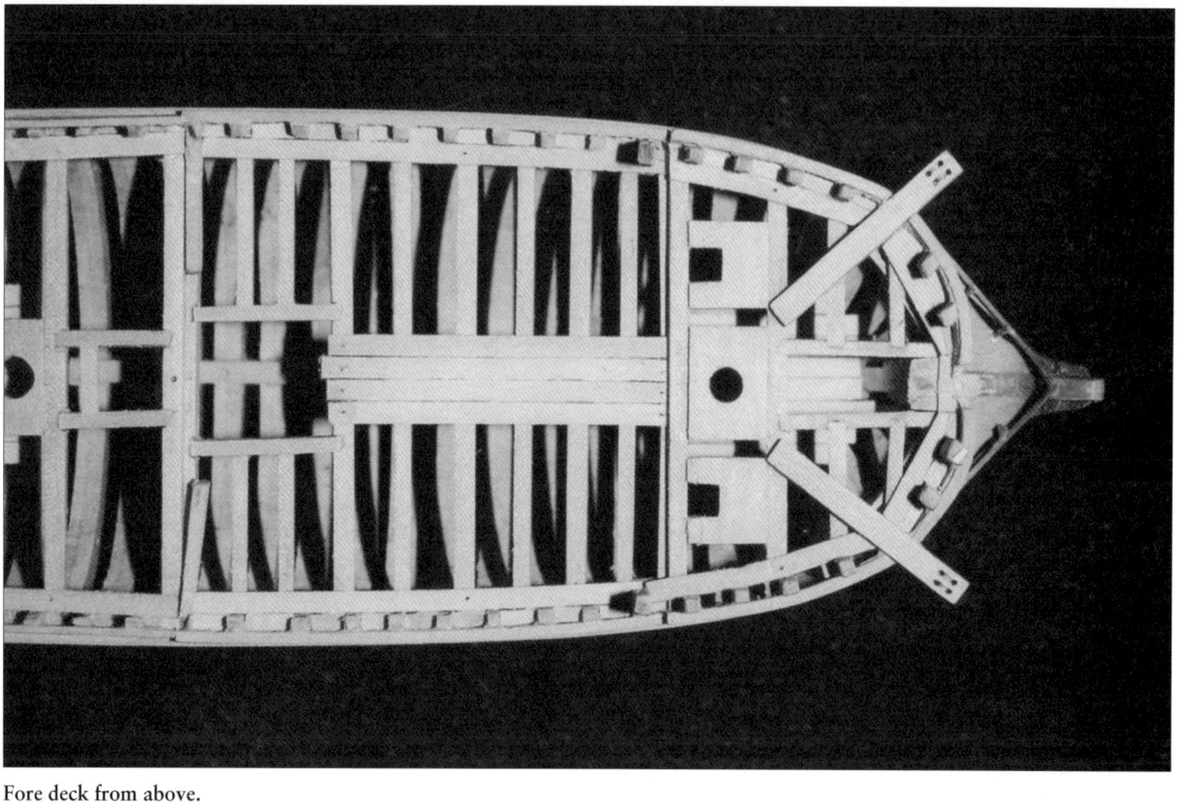

Fore deck from above.

Stern port quarter.

Again using Lyon as a primary reference source the scale of the model can be determined to be at the Imperial scale of 1:96 (⅛in = 1ft). At this scale the model is about 8in (20cm) long. The principal full-size dimensions are:

Length between perpendiculars:
 55ft 6in (16.91m).

Length of keel: 51ft (15.54m).

Maximum beam (measured on the wale): 19ft (5.79m).

Beam to inside of planking: 18ft 6in (5.63m).

Depth from centre of mainmast to top of keelson: 8ft 6in (2.59m).

Forecastle deck: 10ft 6in (3.2m).

Poop deck: 19ft (5.79m).

Centre line of foremast from fore edge of stem: 9ft (2.74m).

Centre line of mainmast from fore edge of stem: 34ft 6in (10.51m).

Distance between centre lines of masts: 25ft 6in (7.77m).

We believe the keel, keelson and framing of the model are of Pearwood, with European Lime being used for the limited planking and possibly the deck beams too (Freeston was a great believer in the modelling qualities of these two timbers – though advised modellers to avoid North American Lime {Basswood} because of its soft, almost furry nature, tendency to blunt tools and be less than amiable in receiving a good finish, though this author's experience of Basswood would suggest otherwise).

Considering the model's relatively small scale the construction methods used are closely copied from full-size practice, demonstrating very high skills levels. The keel is a single piece with the stem, or gripe, scarphed into it. The sternpost is also scarphed into the keel. In both cases the joints are perfectly made. There is no false keel, but these were not

always fitted on such small vessels. The rising wood sits above and between the keel and the sternpost.

The stem is made up of two pieces; the gripe and the bobstay piece, the latter, which also doubles as the main piece (because of the small size of the ship), having a single hole for the bobstay itself and a single gammon slot. As with the gripe into the keel, the gripe and bobstay are also scarphed together.

The fact that this model is predominately unplanked and, except for the wale and transom, unpainted, adds substantially to its beauty because the finely built structure is exposed. The colours of the woods, mellowed by time and light, add to the quality of the craftsmanship and it is through the framing that we can appreciate the work that has gone into this at first seemingly insignificant model. There are twenty-five main frames, each being double as

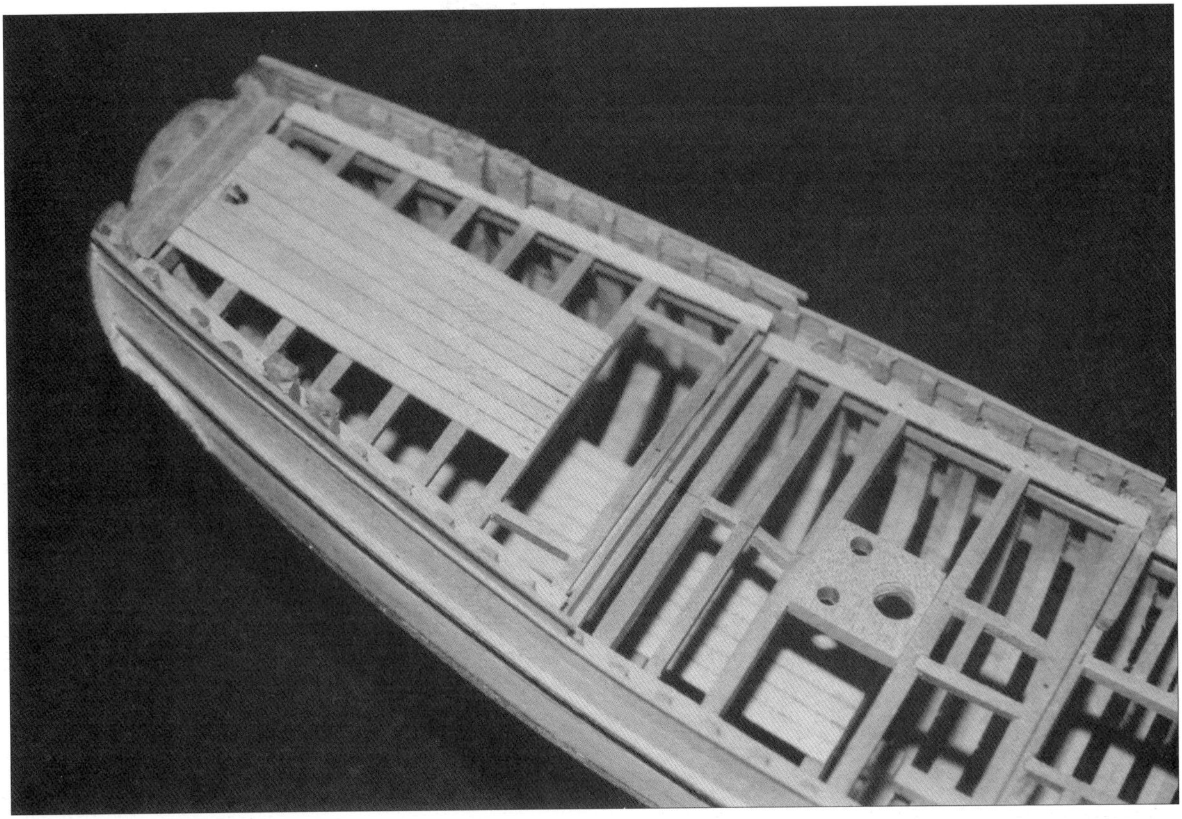

Overhead view of after deck.

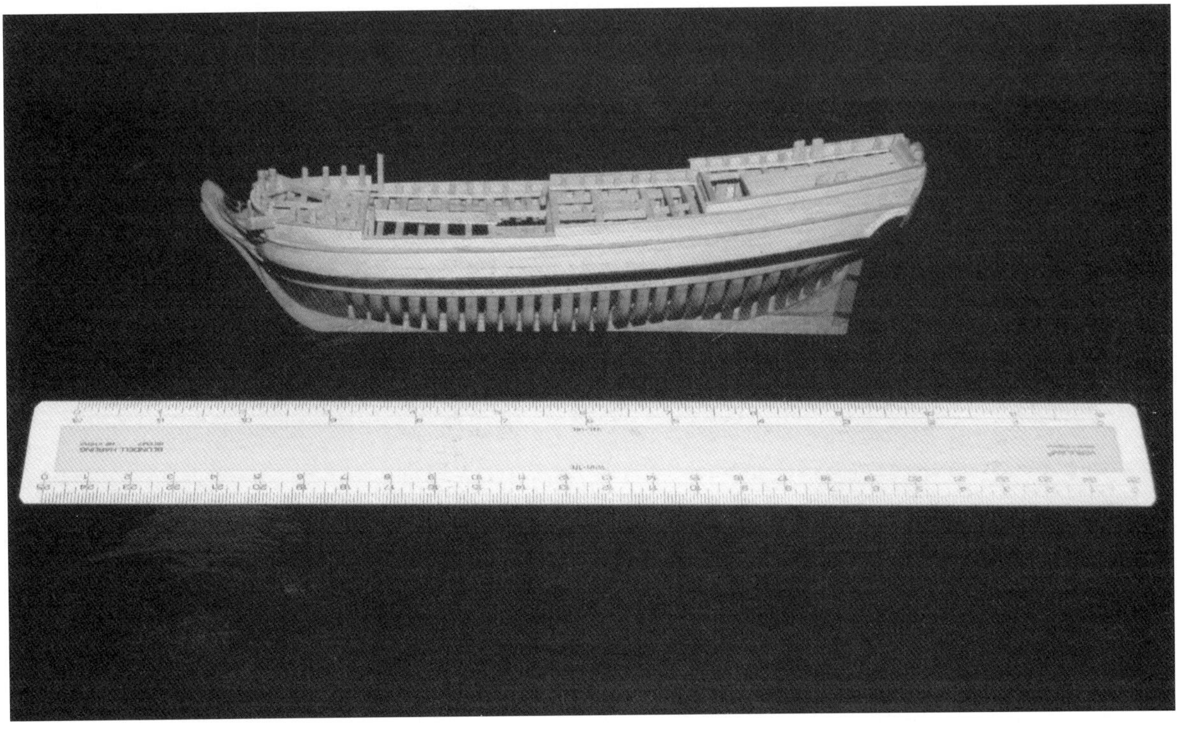

This shows the small size of the hull.

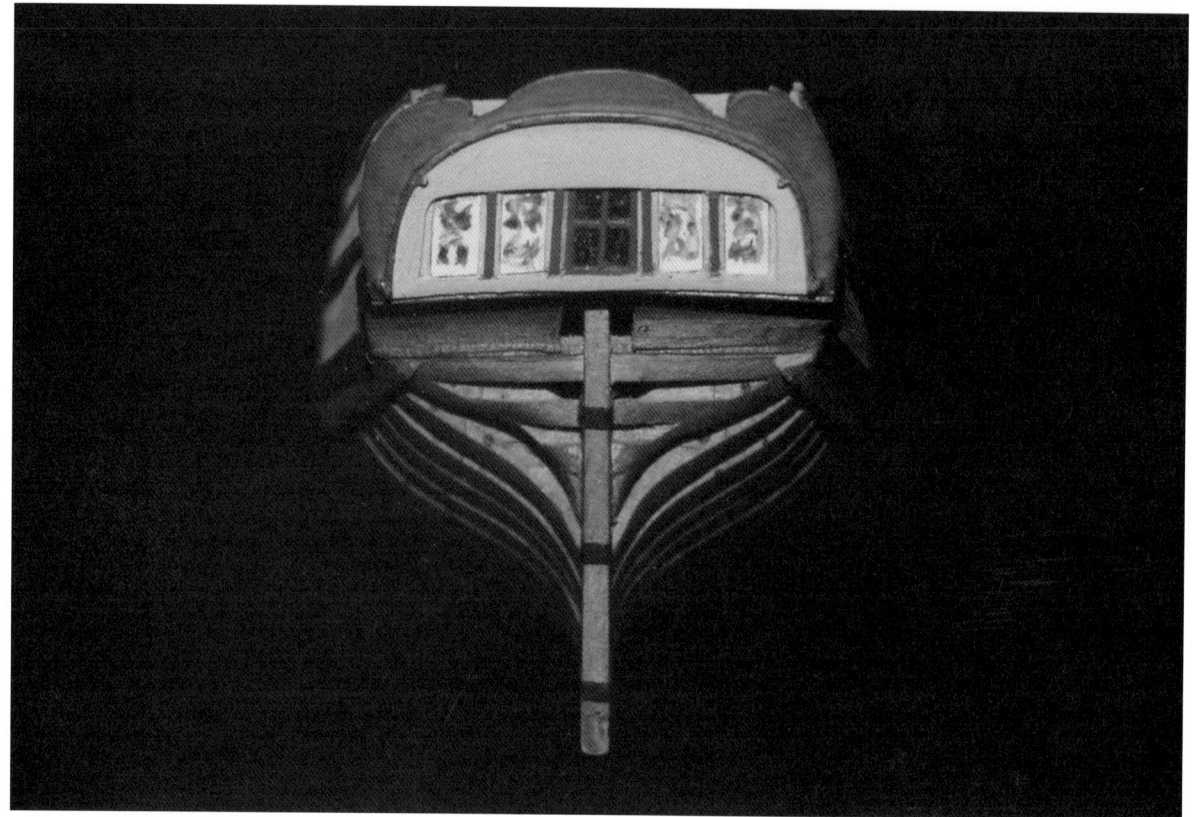

Transom stern detail.

Photographs by the author.

per full-size construction. At full size the frames measure 1ft wide (0.3048m), or 6in for each half. The spacing between frames is approximately 9in (0.255m). Each double frame is made up of five pieces; floor timbers and futtocks. The frames are all drilled and dowelled.

Forward, there are 5.5 cant frames which, as with the square or main frames, are of double construction. Aft there are three cant frames, also double, with one fashion piece and three transom pieces.

The forecastle has two catheads each being drilled and slotted to take the sheaves for the ground tackle ropes. Between the foremast and the main hatch the deck has been planked along the centre line with four planks, whilst the poop has been partially planked with eight planks. These poop planks stop at a large, almost full-width opening which suggests that the design might

well have had a small raised cabin roof at this point (similar to what was often incorporated into small royal yachts built in the seventeenth century.

As previously mentioned the model is only partially planked. The main wale is included and with the transom is the only part of the model to which colour has been applied, in this case black. Below the wale is a single plank which has been drilled and dowelled into each double frame. Above the wale are three side planks which have obviously been steamed to cope with the severe bend forward. However, there is no evidence of any dowelling which is a testament to the steaming process and whichever glue Freeston used. Above these planks is the sheer rail followed by further planks up to and including the forecastle and poop decks. No capping rails are fitted and the inside tops of the frames are

clearly visible above deck levels.

The transom stern shows a single, centrally located window with two false windows either side. These false windows have been decorated with what look like paintings. The transom itself and the mullions between the windows, real and false, have been tinted with Yellow Ochre and Red Ochre respectively.

It is hoped that the beauty and craftsmanship inherent in this model will be evident in the photographs reproduced here. The photographs themselves were taken with a digital SLR (single lens reflex) camera using an 18-85mm lens and a flash attachment. The model was set on a black velvet cloth to maximise detail and contrast, and, by the use of velvet, to avoid reflected light.

If any reader has seen this model in the past and knows something about its history we would be pleased to hear from them. ❏

The Lumberyard for Model Shipwrights

by David Stevens

The beginning

An interest in wood began in the summer of 1979 as part of a newly formed model group named the Great Lakes Society of Model Shipwrights, which was part of the Inland Seas Maritime Museum. The Society began with me (David Stevens) and four other founding members. Two of the more notable were Bob Bruckshaw and Harold Hahn. The society lasted twenty-two years until it finally disbanded. I volunteered at the Museum's library and helped organize the Museum's collection of 1,200 ship plans it had in storage. The society began a modest journal, of which I was the editor. After just a year, I stepped aside as journal editor and headed a service of researching and providing members of the group with modeling wood. It was brought up by our club members to consider buying wood in bulk. Many lumber companies did not stock some of the more exotic wood model-ship builders would like to have used. The reason was that the wood was in such a low demand that it sat around for long periods of time in their stock. So if all the members put in an order for wood perhaps we could persuade a lumber supplier to order the wood for us. That was the beginning of The Lumberyard for Model Shipwrights. I bought bulk and cut the wood down to a workable size for club members.

Collecting

In time, enough different woods were collected that someone suggested I should take the wood collection to a Nautical Research Guild (NRG) conference and sell it there. That started a fifteen-year run of packing up a load of wood and going to NRG conferences. At these conferences I became known as the woodman and my wife as Mrs Wood. Model builders would wait at the van as we unloaded, looking to

1. Slab of steamed pear wood imported from Germany.

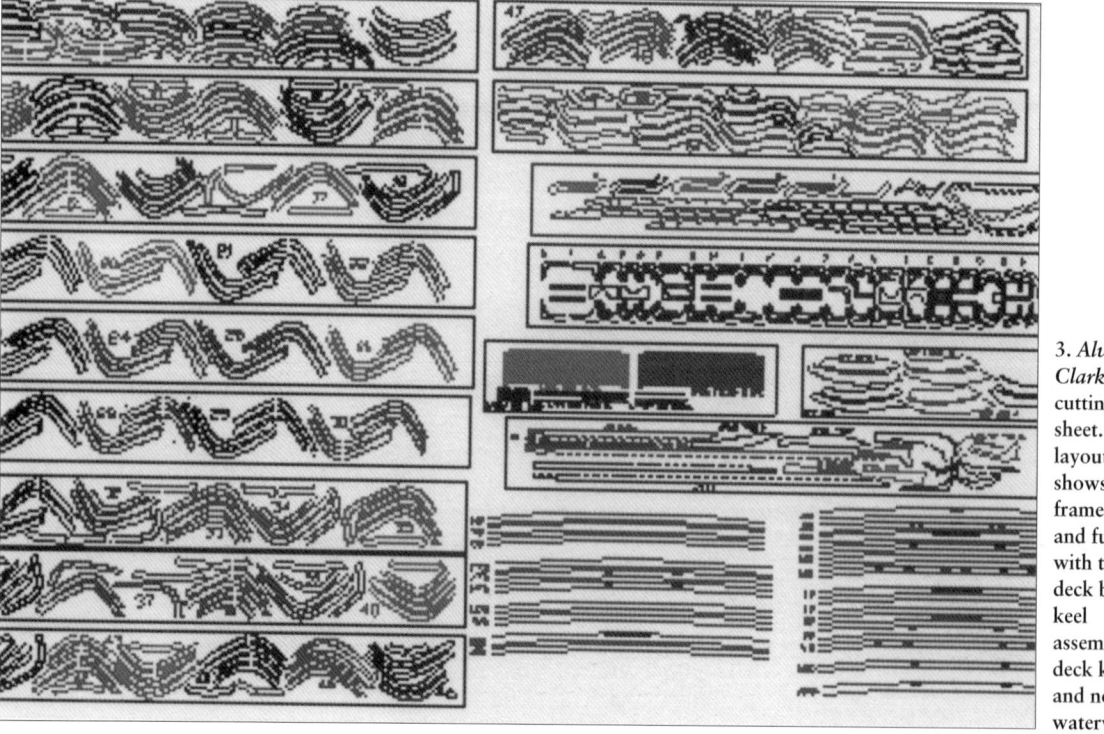

2. American Black Walnut logs being trimmed and prepared to be taken to the sawmill.

3. *Alvin Clark* cutting sheet. This layout shows every frame, floor and futtock, with the deck beams, keel assembly, deck knees and notched waterways.

grab the best pieces. As word spread of the collection of wood we had at the NRG conferences we began to advertise in the local newspaper – trees wanted dead or alive. I would go out in my van with a chain saw and bring home all kinds of logs. I kicked around the idea of going into the lumber business and calling it Dragon Wood because I was always dragging home another log of something or another. But the name The Lumberyard for Model Shipwrights seemed more appropriate.

Milling

In the early years the Lumberyard supplied only bulk wood. Millwork came a few years later. Taking the chance we invested in the necessary machines and built a workshop behind the house. Soon after advertising the availability of milled wood, the demand skyrocketed. Thousands and thousands of milled

sheets and strip wood became the major focus of the company. In the first photograph is a slab of steamed pear wood imported from Germany; in the second photograph are American Black Walnut logs being trimmed and prepared ready to be taken to the sawmill.

At one conference my wife and I met a man, Milt Roth, who started a mail order ship model supply company. Milt and I hit it off and spent the next two years and many hours talking about ship modeling. Milt saw a void between the hobby kits being offered and the serious scratch builders. I told Milt that our club members were buying kits, throwing out the wood and having me mill quality replacement wood. What if a high-quality plank-on-frame kit could be produced?

The timbering set

Over the years I had always kept in

contact with Harold Hahn. The next time I saw Harold, I asked him if I could make a kit from his plans. A problem at hand for a model builder is the lack of machines to mill out the wood. This is an expensive investment. Another problem is locating wood in small amounts. This gave rise to the concept of a semi-kit. The builder would be provided with the high quality milled wood, laser cut framing jig and a few select parts along with a set of Harold's plans. Harold agreed with the idea and the timbering set was born. The timbering set started a twenty-year business relationship with Harold Hahn, his plans and the Lumberyard's milled and laser cut wood parts.

Computer design

Along with the milling and production of the Hahn timbering sets the Lumberyard's next endeavor was

4. *Alvin Clark.*

computer design. In conjunction with Steve Owen at Double O Laser and Jim Roberts of North River Scale Models the concept of a computer-generated model was conceived. Between the three companies we produced the first true plank-on-frame ship model kit. The concept of computer drafting a hull then disassembling it into its component parts and creating a CNC cutting program was my brain child. Jim Roberts worked on the creation of the kits and Steve perfected the precision laser cutting that was needed. Two concept kits were under development the *Diligence* and the *Oneida*. The untimely death of Jim Roberts put a sudden end to the project.

Full time

For a long time the Lumberyard remained a part-time business while I pursued a twenty-eight year career in commercial art. I began as a glass sculptor then a graphic artist. I was a photographer, a printer, a package designer, a product developer, a draftsman and an illustrator. When it all became overwhelming, I left commercial art in the early nineties. My brother Carl and I joined up and started a tree removal business. Here I found a source for literally tons and tons of logs. Living within the boundaries of North America's hardwood forest and between my woodworking knowledge and Carl's horticultural education we were able to identify and select types of wood suitable for fine model building from a literal cornucopia of trees. As a model-shipbuilder myself, I was able to select wood for its color, texture and properties. I could then introduce to model-builders woods they never thought of using. Rather than cut the trees into firewood, my brother and I got involved in sawmills and logging. When my brother sold the tree business, I had no desire to get back into the commercial arts. It was time for the Lumberyard to become a full-time business. Continuing to add to the selection of native timbers, the Lumberyard enlarged its contacts and network of importers and wood dealers from North to South America and across the world. Development of the plank-on-frame kit was set on the back burner and attention was directed to logging, sawmill lumbering and millwork. The Lumberyard continued to grow into an international business supplying wood to model builders all over the world. Today the company maintains an ever changing inventory of over 120 types of wood. There are those traditional woods that were always associated with ship modeling dating back to the builders of the Admiralty model. These woods such as Boxwood and Pearwood are

5. A diorama scene aboard the schooner *Halifax*, built by Harold Hahn.

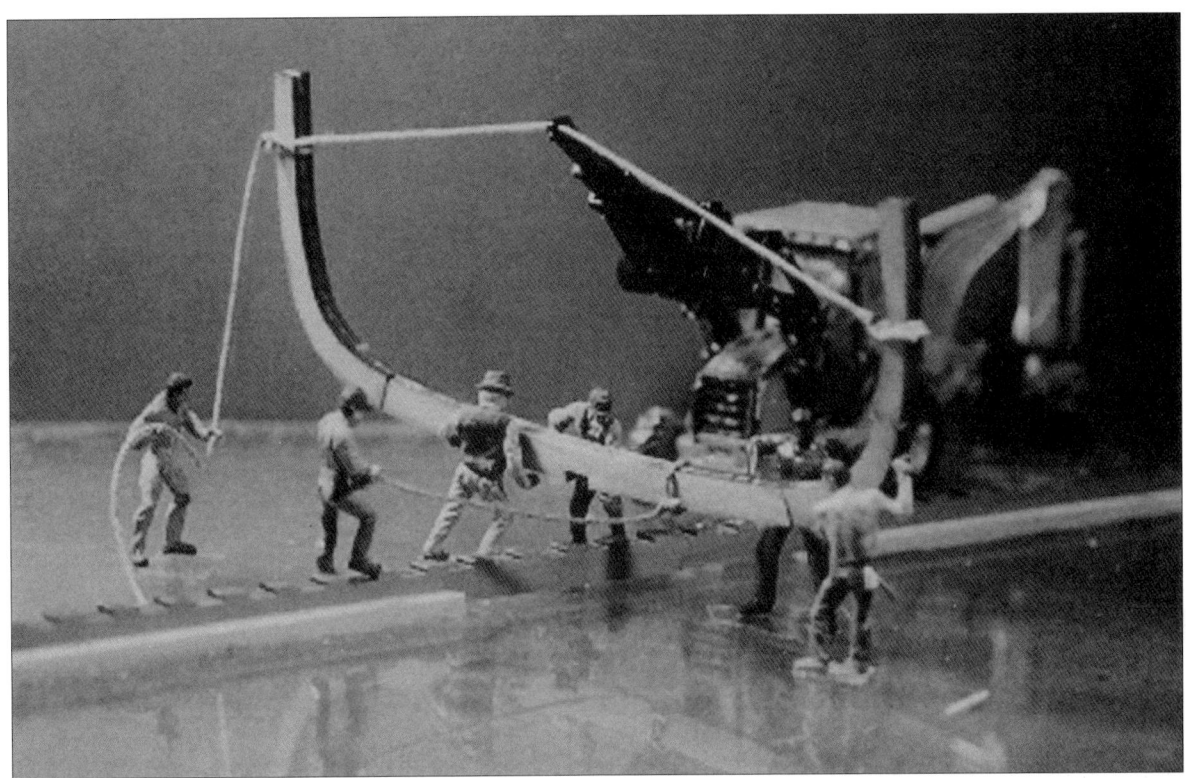

6. A crew setting up the first frame of the *Alvin Clark*.

always part of the inventory and sources are constantly sought after and maintained.

As business grew beyond the ability for one man to operate, my wife jumped in to help. She is my right arm, my left arm, my memory bank. She does all the paperwork, the customer service, the follow-ups. She is the one who keeps the customers coming back. She is the complaint department, the answering service, the bookkeeper. Without her 'help' the Lumberyard would be in dire straights. With Mrs Wood now running the business I found a little time to focus on research and development. The idea of a true plank-on-frame kit was dusted off and re-examined. After the development of the prototype plank-on-frame kit of the *Oneida*, a typical Great Lakes schooner was developed based on the shipwreck of the *Alvin Clark*. A kit was designed timber for timber just as the original ship was built. Back in the days of learning how to

draft a set of ship plans with Bob Bruckshaw, by hand, on a drafting table, with the traditional tools of the trade, the process was a long and tedious one. The introduction of computer-aided drafting took model ship plans to a whole new level. It became apparent an entire ship could be modeled on the computer. Each timber could be separated and laid out into a cutting file for a CNC operation.

Alvin Clark

By using computer drafting and a laser with a + or − of 0.003 to cut out the parts, it might be thought that anyone could assemble a ship model straight away like putting together a jigsaw puzzle. Not so; by creating absolutely perfect parts there was no room left for assembly error. The very nature of wood is that it will move, expand and shrink. The hand of man also introduces slight errors, which add up and produce a distorted model. A solution to

the assembly problem was to make the individual parts slightly oversize, thus giving the builder some latitude so the parts could be shaped or sized to fit into the model at whatever stage of construction it has reached.

With the introduction of CDs, with the bugs worked out of the plank-on-frame kit, it became clear that instruction would be necessary. This led to a new phase for the Lumberyard, the building instruction CDs. Back in the 1980s while a member of the Great Lakes Society of Model Shipwrights, I had the opportunity to learn from two well-seasoned builders, Bob Bruckshaw and Harold Hahn. Bob Bruckshaw tutored me in the fine art of model-ship building (see *MS11* and *MS12* for an article by Harold Hahn about Bob Bruckshaw model maker), and Harold Hahn inspired me with his use of figures and the diorama setting. The first instructions on building the *Oneida* dealt primarily with the assembly of the model. A second

CD on the building of the *Alvin Clark* incorporated diorama scenes.

The scenes were not permanent dioramas but merely set up and photographed then taken apart and construction of the model would resume. I felt it helped visualize the construction of the model.

Photographs 5 and 6 are my visual aid dioramas . Photograph 6 is of a crew setting up the first frame of the *Alvin Clark*. It is a combination of how to build the model and a diorama of how a frame might have been set if a wooden ship was being built in modern times adds interest to the CD. The models are built on a piece of ¼in plate glass to keep everything flat and level. Harold Hahn expertly carved his figures. Rather than carve my own or search for period figures, the diorama is set in such a way that any scale figures could be used to demonstrate building a wooden ship. I know this may be considered cheating in some quar-

ters, but the focus was to be educational. The dioramas depict the 1840 wooden schooner being built by a crew in 2008. The dark color on the edge of the frames is a laser residue left on the surface of the wood as a result of the cutting process, and it can be sanded off quite easily.

In some cases props, such as scaffolding, can be built and added to the diorama. It would have been helpful to have had a crane in 1840, but seeing that the *Alvin Clark* is being built in 2008 a crane is available to help set the transom timber. In Photograph 10 some of the figures have been coaxed into postures so they look ntural in the scene. Arms are bent or cut off and re-attached in a different position. With the small work crews swarming all over the model, it became apparent that to produce this type of instructional CD required five times the effort and the addition of many more hours work. It was fun but too time-con-

suming. After the completion of the *Alvin Clark* project the diorama approach was abandoned in favour of the simpler style of the basic how to build a model.

Hull construction

A couple of methods were tried to assemble a hull accurately from laser cut parts. One method was to build the hull in a jig system developed by Harold Hahn. Another method was to build free form. The jig method worked up to a point. The jig kept the framing in place, but did not guarantee an accurately built hull. Frames still could be slanted fore and aft along with tilting from side to side. The jig method worked to the point where the hull had to be cut loose and all remaining parts had to be right. Another method, introduced by Portia Takakjian, was to use what she referred to as packing pieces between the frames at the level of the wales. From an archaeological

7. The use of figures in a diorama.

8. One of the work crew.

first frame on a flat surface, then add a block on top of the frame at the bulwarks and one at the centre of the floor. Next, add another frame on top of the block to build up sections of about five frames. These frame sections are then assembled into the hull. Looking at Photograph 10 of a crew planking the bulwarks, the filler blocks between the frames can be seen. Because the bulwarks are not planked on the inside, the filler blocks are set at the level of the deck clamp where the hull planking will cover them.

Now what?

The Lumberyard is not a company with a large staff of employees and multiple departments for research and development, logging and mill-work, or design and drafting. The problem of expansion was solved by the creation of a network of companies, individuals, other websites, and

report of the warship *Jefferson* it was noted that additional pieces of wood were fastened between the top timbers, making the bulwark a solid wall of timber. The use of chocks or filler blocks between the frames seemed to be a viable method. A variation to this method is to set the

9. Stern frames being set up by work crew.

organizations. This results in a symbiotic relationship where everyone involved works as a team to bring to the ship modeling community state of the art ideas and products. This was first tried with the *Lexington* project. The creator developed the project then published the historical background in one journal, the building process in a modeling magazine, and then created a live on-line builder's forum. The Lumberyard created the semi-kit. The *Lexington* project proved to be the first successful multi-media project, which combines a magazine, a journal, an on-line builder's forum, a laser cutting company and a lumber company. With this idea in mind, the Lumberyard teamed up with another web site and an on-line publication *Model Ship Builder* to design a kit of John Cabot's ship the *Matthew*, a caravel of 1479. The Lumberyard is also involved in an Australian-based

site to offer on-line classes in how to develop plank-on-bulkhead as well as plank-on-frame ship plans. The subject of the classes is a British gunboat, the *Caustic*, built on Lake Champlain in North America. This project will eventually develop into a fully laser cut kit and an on-line building project. In the works and on the drawing board, is a story about William Bell, born in 1777 in Fifeshire, Scotland, who entered employment for the Provincial Marine in Canada as naval shipwright at the age of 22. Bell built the warship fleet on Lake Erie and later was appointed Master Shipwright at the Admiralty shipyard at Kingston, Canada, where he built one of the largest first-rate warships of its time. Bell was replaced by Thomas Strickland as Master Shipwright at Kingston but remained Strickland's assistant. One of Bell's ships, the *General Hunter*, was found and the

Lumberyard is working with the archaeological information to recreate the ship. Another project in the works is the frigate *Psyche*, built at Chatham yard in Kent, England, then taken apart and sent to the Kingston yard in Canada were it was reassembled. The unique design of the *Psyche* was a one-of-a-kind frigate with a sharp V-bottom hull.

Under the direction and guidance of the companies chief executive officer, the project mentioned above will be developed into historical articles, model-building articles, modeling plans and state of the art plank-on-frame kits. The Lumberyard and its associates will continue developing new ideas, kits and articles in both print and E publishing along with the continued services of millwork. As we move forward into the future our chief executive officer and leader has made our objective clear, 'We don't follow trends we set them'. ❑

10. Scaffolding has been added.

11. & 12. Showing aspects of the construction of the hull.

Photographs by the author.

The Scottish Zulu *Muirneag* SY486, 1903–1947

(Part 2)

by Gordon Williams

A few deck beams were put in next, in selected positions, to give rigidity without restricting access for the interior detail. These beams were cambered, and their ends were half-housed to the frames and on to the shelf. This was a strip of pearwood running round the inside of the frames. The wales were then fitted, tight under the rails and on top of the planking. The shape of the wale is interesting, twisting from the vertical at midships to around 60 degrees at the stern, and of course following the deck line in both planes. Again, much steam and patience was required to obtain a satisfactory fit.

The dowels for the planks were American Black Walnut, sawn to around 0.8mm square (on my miniature Proxxon table saw) then pulled through a series of diminishing-sized holes in a drawplate. A discarded cabinet scraper in which a suitable series of holes have been drilled is fine for this. The dowels finished at 0.6mm diameter, and were cut off in 6mm lengths. Later I counted the dowels in the hull, and ended up with a total of 2,800 or so. After the planking came the job of sanding the hull. Using various shaped blocks, and progressing from

Poop deck with stem capstan, boiler and stove flue, foremast crutch and warp room cover.

Port side, showing part of the massive sail area.

100 grit down to 240 grit, the hull slowly revealed her curves; to view the run of the planking from stem to stern is one of the great pleasures of this business.

Finishing the hull

When I was satisfied with the outcome (and much relieved to see just a few tiny gaps in the planking) the stem iron was fitted around the keel. In the full-sized boat, this 1in thick iron strip protected the keel and stem when grounding. I made it from several strips of ½in aluminium, pinned to the stem, keel and sternpost, with flattened ends pinned to the bow and stern breasthooks. The cutout area in the starboard hull planking was tidied up, along with the cut ends of the frame timberheads, and the rubbing strakes were fitted. These were made from ⅛in aluminium sheet, the edge

filed to half-round section then ripped off on the saw, and fixed on to the walnut bedding strips with brass pins. On the port side the rubbing strakes (and the two rows of protective iron belting on the main wale each side) are walnut and painted.

Interior detail

From the drawings, and the photographs of the Zulu *Research* (at the Fisheries Museum, Anstruther, Fife, Scotland) I had a very good record of the inside of the cabin. The first step was to form the ceiling – the boarding on the inside of the frames on the port side behind the bunks. Then the bunk bases and partitions were made and fitted. The front frame with its sliding doors (though not sliding on the model) was made up from strips of 0.6mm lime glued on to a veneer base, and fixed on top of the bench seat. The mattresses for the bunks were tissue paper wrapped around a flat strip of wood, and soaked with paint. The tissue expands and crumples as the paint dries, giving a good representation of bedding. Cherry was used for the cabin floorboards, and they were partly covered with card painted to look like linoleum. The ladder, which was made in walnut, together with various lockers and shelves, completed the woodwork. The donkey boiler, stove and fittings were made up from walnut, ebony and various metals, with the fabrication of the miniature gauges and handwheel being particularly challenging. The handwheels (there is also one on top of the capstan) were made from ¹⁄₁₆in square brass, machined with a fly-cutter in the lathe to form a cross in section, then soldered to a ³⁄₃₂in diameter brass ring, and turned off to leave a short spigot. The fish hold was next, with its walnut stanchions and remov-

Stern, showing steering chains.

Foredeck, with foresail tack hook.

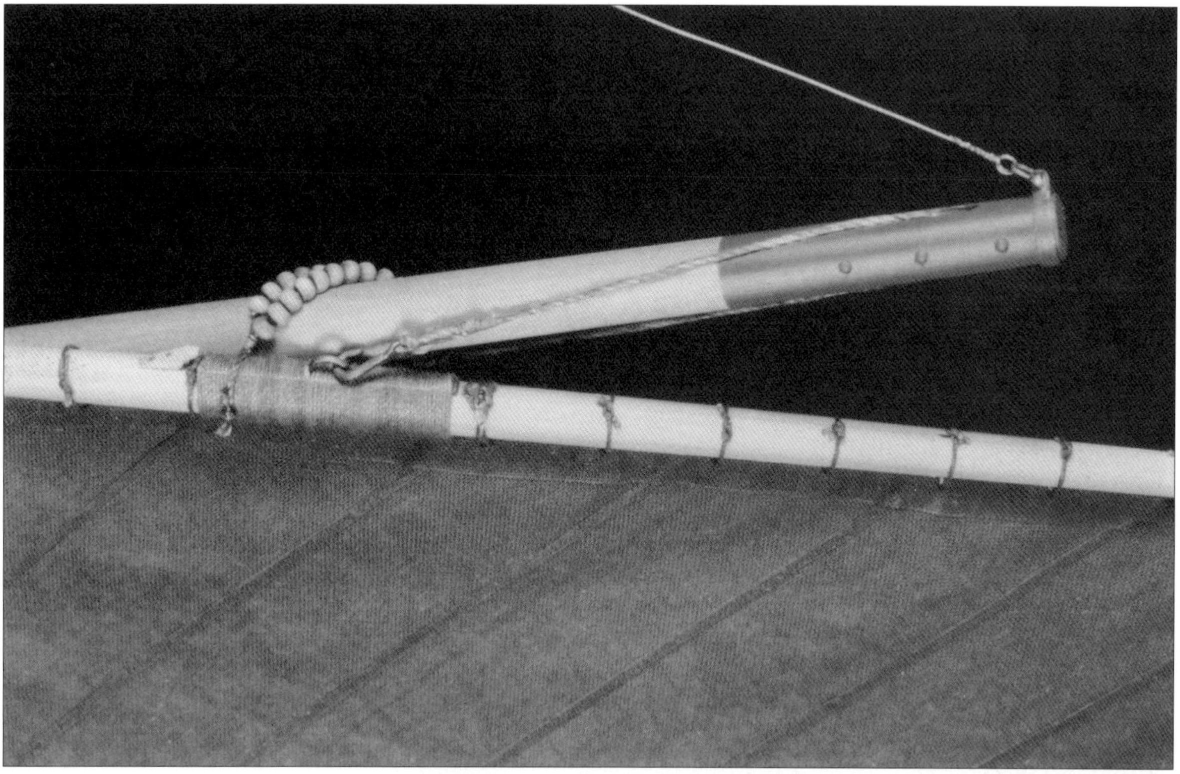

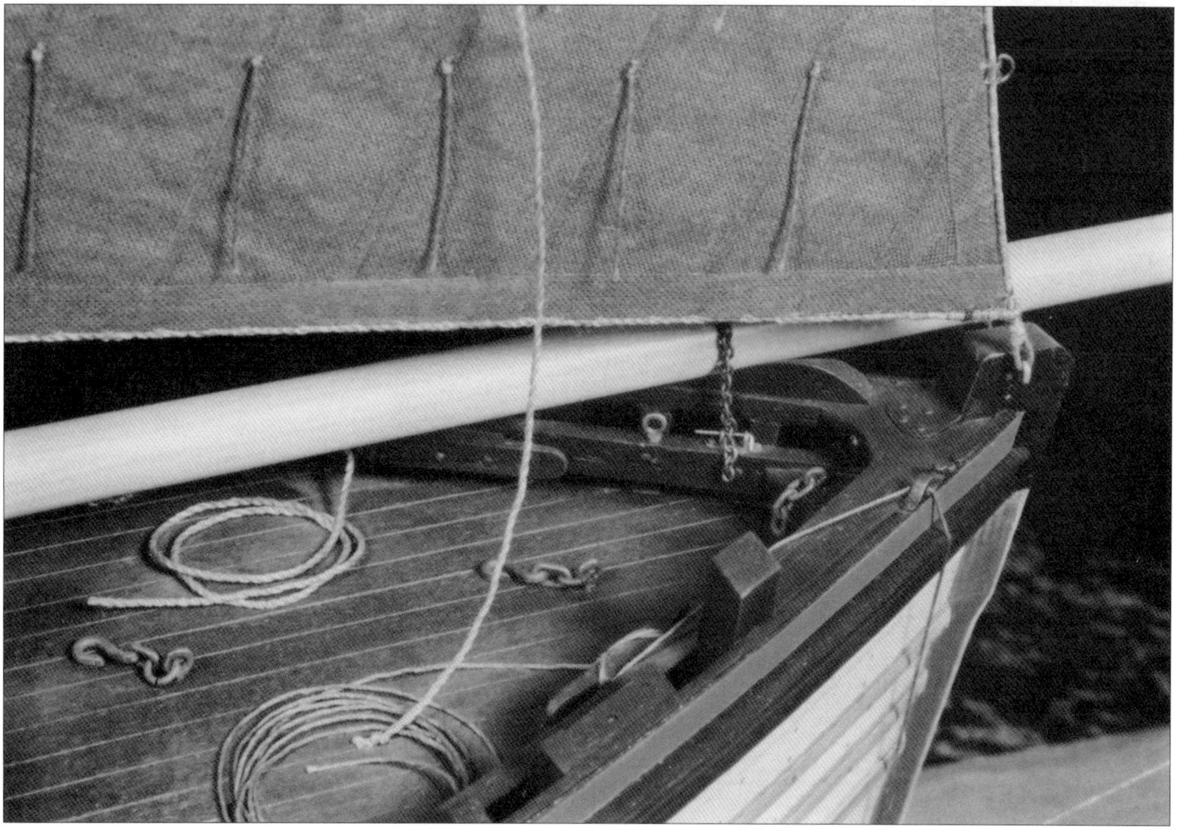

able dividing boards, which were made from limewood. These boards gave the skipper control over where he stored his catch, and allowed him to trim the boat. The removable net platform on top of the hold held the wet nets after the fish were stored. The forecastle shelving was meant to be full of all sorts of tackle and gear, but time caught up with me. The emptiness of these shelves, however, allows the frames and planks of the port side to be seen.

The mast box is framed in the middle of the floor, and allowed the foremast to be lowered back on to the crutch, when the boat was drifting with the nets out (to prevent the very heavy mainmast setting up a pendulum motion which could damage the nets). All the interior woodwork was then given two coats of a tung-based oil, brushed on and the surplus wiped off with a rag after a few minutes, which gave a superb satin finish. When all the

interior was finished, the remaining deck beams and carlings – longitudinal beams, to take short crossbeams – were fitted. The deck was planked with cherry boards, pinned with around 1,100 walnut dowels. As the boards would be painted black, the minimal amount of chamfer was put on their edges to allow the joints to show; this is visually more satisfying than a flat, featureless expanse of deck, and gives a fair approximation of the caulking of the 2in yellow pine boards. The deck was planked from the centre board outwards, after the infill margin planks were fitted between the timberheads. The poop deck was framed up and planked, and the underside, which forms the cabin roof, painted white.

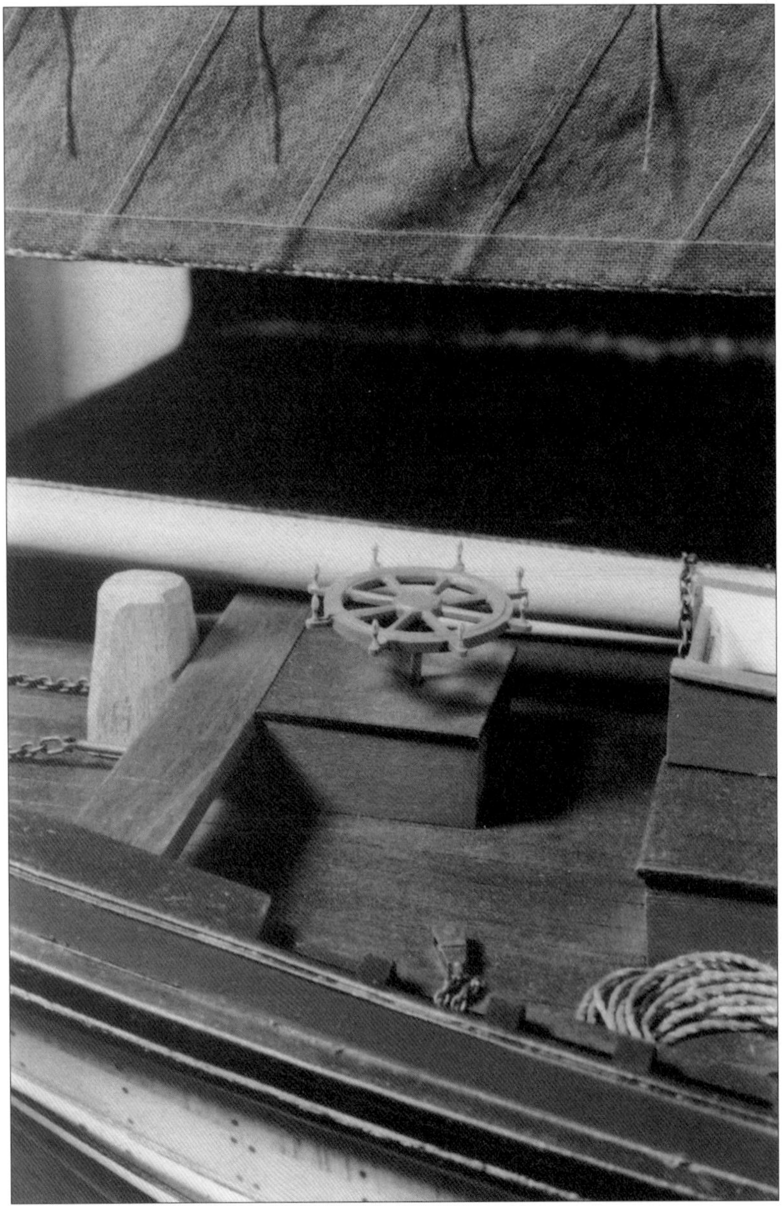

External fittings

The rudder was jointed from walnut boards and hung on pintles and straps (gudgeons) made from brass, silver-soldered together for strength and neatness. Most of the finished brass fittings were chemically darkened to look like iron. This was done by submerging them in old used photographic fixer, the older the better. For a possible source of supply, try a local photography club, they throw the stuff away (it may, however, be rarer in this digital age). This turns the brass to grey/black after a few minutes. If left to harden, this chemical coating is quite tough, although a coat of matt varnish improves its durability. The horizontal wheel was cut from a turned disc of brass, pierced and filed to shape, with the small turned handles fixed on and polished. This involved a lot of very careful and difficult filing, but this was easier than the other methods I tried. The steam capstan was made up from brass, stainless steel, copper, aluminium and walnut, and glued temporarily on a stick for ease of

General view of after deck, horizontal wheel and cabin companionway on right.

assembly and painting. The chimneys for the boiler and stove were made from brass tubing, silver-soldered. On the foredeck the heavy, tapering skegs which support the foremast were pinned to the deck together with their knees, and corresponding boltheads fitted under the deck beams. The nets are from net curtaining, stained black. It was difficult to find the correct scale size to correspond to the full-size 1in mesh, which would only catch fish of the correct size and maturity. Net floats were fitted into the side wings of the fish hold (made from beech and painted) and the loose hatch boards stacked forward of the hold. The net rope (or warp) can also be seen, going over the roller into the warp room. This rope is left-hand (cable) laid, which gives more flexibility to a large rope.

Painting and oiling

Much of the interior was painted or oiled before the hull was planked, which forced a strict regime of dust protection. This was nothing more than the internal spaces being filled with very soft tissue, but of course dust has a special ability where small parts are concerned, and much time was spent with a blower brush (for camera lenses) and other very small and soft brushes, cleaning out the corners. The port side of the hull was sealed with one coat of oil, then airbrushed in Liquitex Artist's Acrylic, which is flexible and non-fading. A primer coat of grey was followed by several coats of the correct white, brick-red and black. For masking the white cutwater, extremely thin self-adhesive metal foil was used, and great care was needed to get the line sweeping correctly; foil is not the easiest thing to use, and I had to join it in several places. This was not easy, as the joins had to be perfect. The resulting paint edge, however, was excellent and well worth the extra effort. The deck was brush painted in black, one coat only, to allow the surface texture of the

planks to show through. The vessel's name and number were first outlined in white ink with a drawing pen, then filled in with acrylic. With the painting done, the model was mounted temporarily on a baseboard while the masts and rigging were fitted.

Masting and sails

Masts and spars are of Lemonwood (Degame, apparently very close to Lancewood; Degame/Lemonwood is often referred to as Lancewood), which is truly wonderful for the job. It is very close-grained, takes a beautiful finish, and most importantly stays perfectly straight. The masts and booms were shaped by hand, tapering them first in square section and then to eight-sided and sixteen-sided, before scraping with semi-circular scrapers. They were finish-sanded with 320 grit paper,

Skegs, and wedge supporting the foremast.

Heel of bowsprit clamped and pinned to fore thwart.

Stern in the building jig, with steel band riveted on head of sternpost.

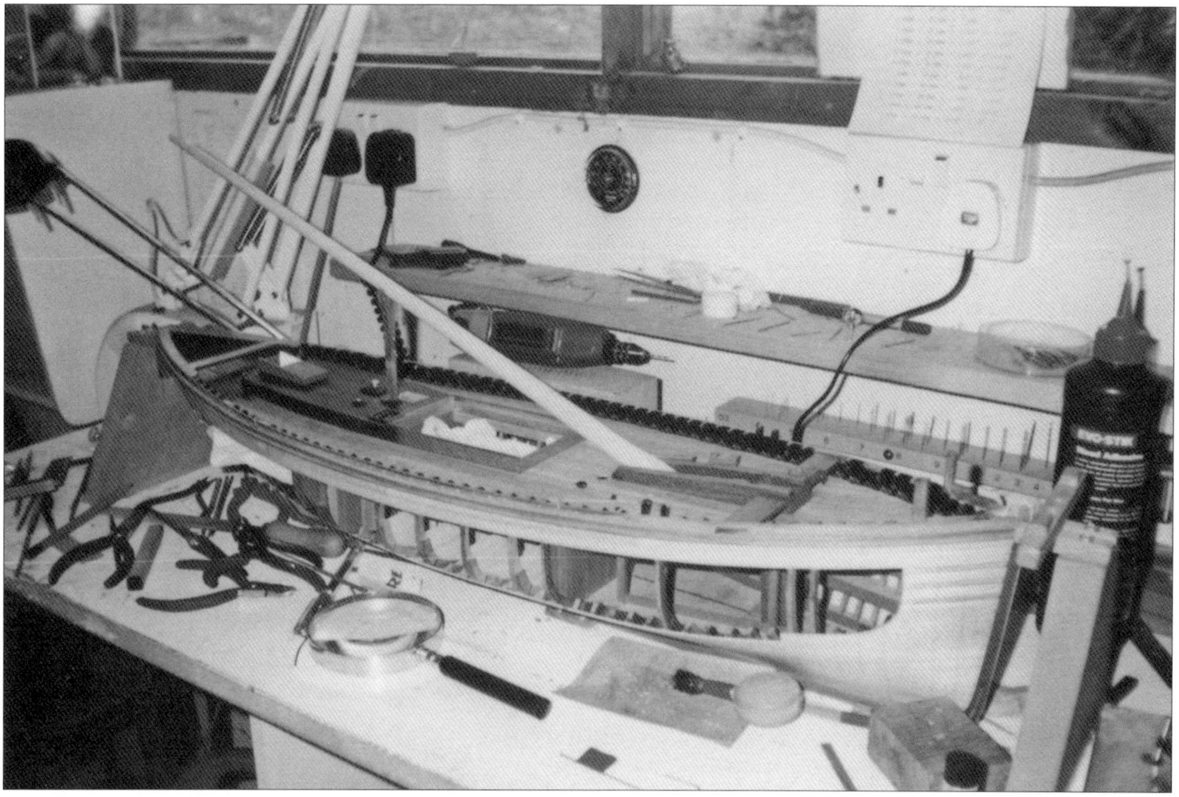

Hull in the assembly jig, with foremast lowered on to the crutch.

Starboard deck, showing oars and the 'wands' used for pushing the boat out from its mooring.

and oiled to a glass-like finish. The sails were cotton cambric, hot-dyed, ironed flat and cut to the shape of card templates. I was unhappy with my options regarding stitching as the machine, or hand stitches I was capable of producing, would be oversize even at this scale. So I decided not to stitch the seams. The only hand-stitching was to fix the bolt-ropes around the outside edges of the sails. The seams and hems were represented by strips of fabric glued to the sails with PVA. These hems were stiffened by brushing with a weak PVA solution, and when dry cut with a knife and straightedge to produce sharp-edged

Interior of cabin before the poop deck was fitted.

non-fraying strips. The wire ropes on the luffs of the main and mizzen sails were served with yarn, on a simple contraption with rotating hooks at each end, made from plastic tubing and gears.

Having seen so many models with reefs sticking out unhappily at all angles from the sails, I was determined to do something better. However, try as I did, knotting them through then trying to flatten them against the sails was unsuccessful. My final method was simply to glue the dyed and knotted ropes directly to each side of the sail fabric, and I felt this was visually successful.

Supporting the model

I prefer the stand/support arrangement to be discreet, and not detract from the model. All the models I have made have been mounted on quite delicate-looking pedestals, turned from mahogany or brass, and fixed by long screws up through the keel and into the bulkheads. With *Muirneag*, the centre fixing is an M5 bolt going into a threaded plate firmly fixed out of sight, between frames 23 and 24. The two other mountings are 4.5mm drill shanks, which locate into brass tubes in the hull. All a bit 'belt and braces' it may seen, but on a biggish model I prefer to be safe. The final touch was an etched brass nameplate giving the basic details of the boat, fixed on the baseboard off the starboard bow.

The model took more than a year to build. It can be seen in much greater detail at www.muirneag.net.

Muirneag is now the property of Museum nan Eilean (The Museum of the Western Isles) at Francis Street, Stornoway, and may be viewed there. ❑

Starboard bow, with bobstay, jib outhaul running over a sheave on the stem.

The complete model of *Muirneag*.

Photographs by the author.

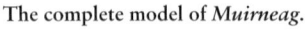

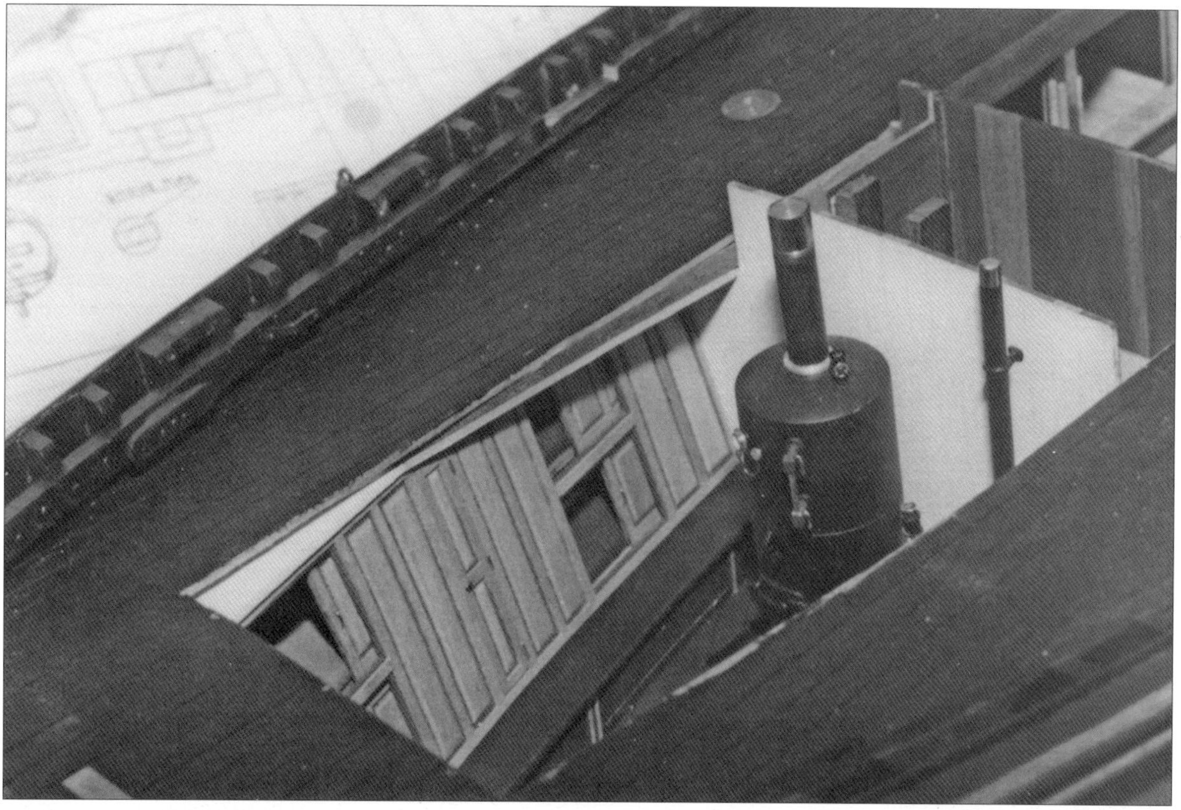

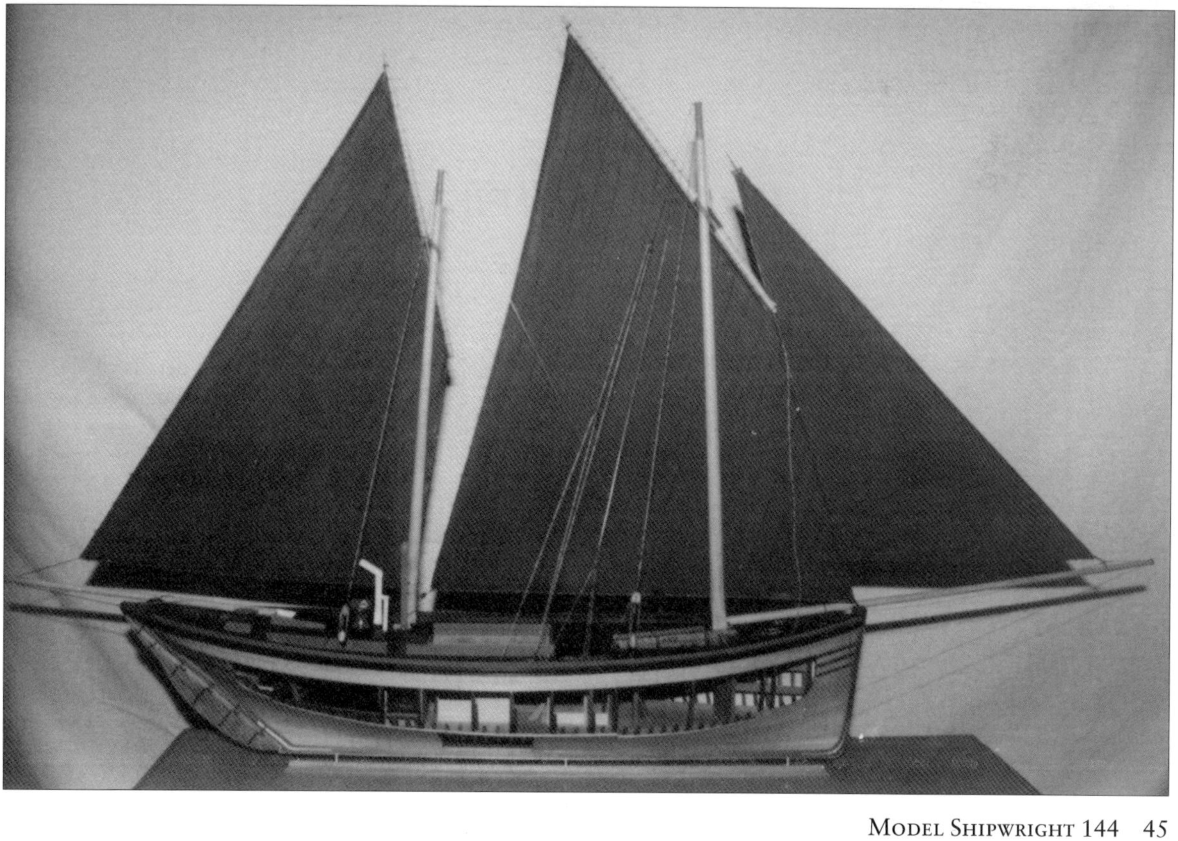

Braemar Castle (1898)

by R A Wilson

History

The *Braemar Castle* was completed in 1898 by Barclay, Curle, Glasgow for the Castle Line. She was an intermediate steamer of 6,266 gross tons with a length of 450ft and a beam of 52.2ft. Powered by a quadruple expansion engine, the service speed was 13.5 knots, although at trials, she achieved a speed of 15.3 knots.

She was the first of the company vessels not to be fitted with square sails although a total of nine fore-and-aft sails could be carried on the four masts. She was also the last single-screw passenger vessel built for the company. When I joined the company late in 1965, there were still serving officers who remembered the older passenger liners setting sail in the event of engine failure, but, by all accounts, they were not very effective even in high winds and only provided steerage way at best. Sails had generally been dispensed with long before the start of World War Two. Despite the fact that the *Braemar Castle* lasted for twenty-four years she only ran for about eleven years in the service for which she was built. In about 1900, the Castle and Union lines combined to form the famous Union-Castle Mail Steamship Company. In 1902, the *Braemar Castle* went ashore on the Isle of Wight for a couple of days, but received no serious damage. In 1909, she was chartered by the British Government for use as a troopship, and was painted white with a blue band round the hull and a yellow funnel. This service continued until the outbreak of World War One, during which she carried the British Expeditionary Force to France in 1914. The following year, 1915, found the ship carrying troops to Gallipoli, after which she was refitted as a 421-bed hospital ship.

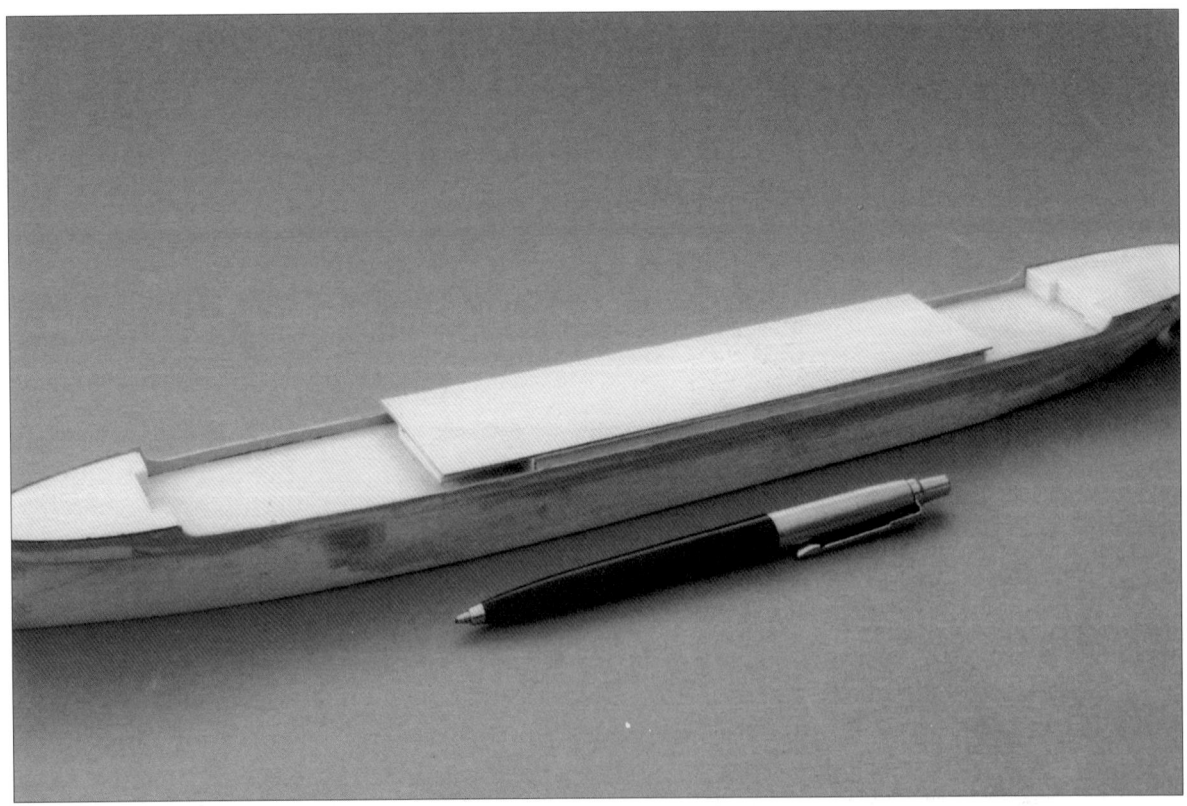

The basic hull has been fitted with the bulwarks. Each was put on as a single piece between forecastle and poop, running along, and being glued to, the lower part of the side of the midship island.

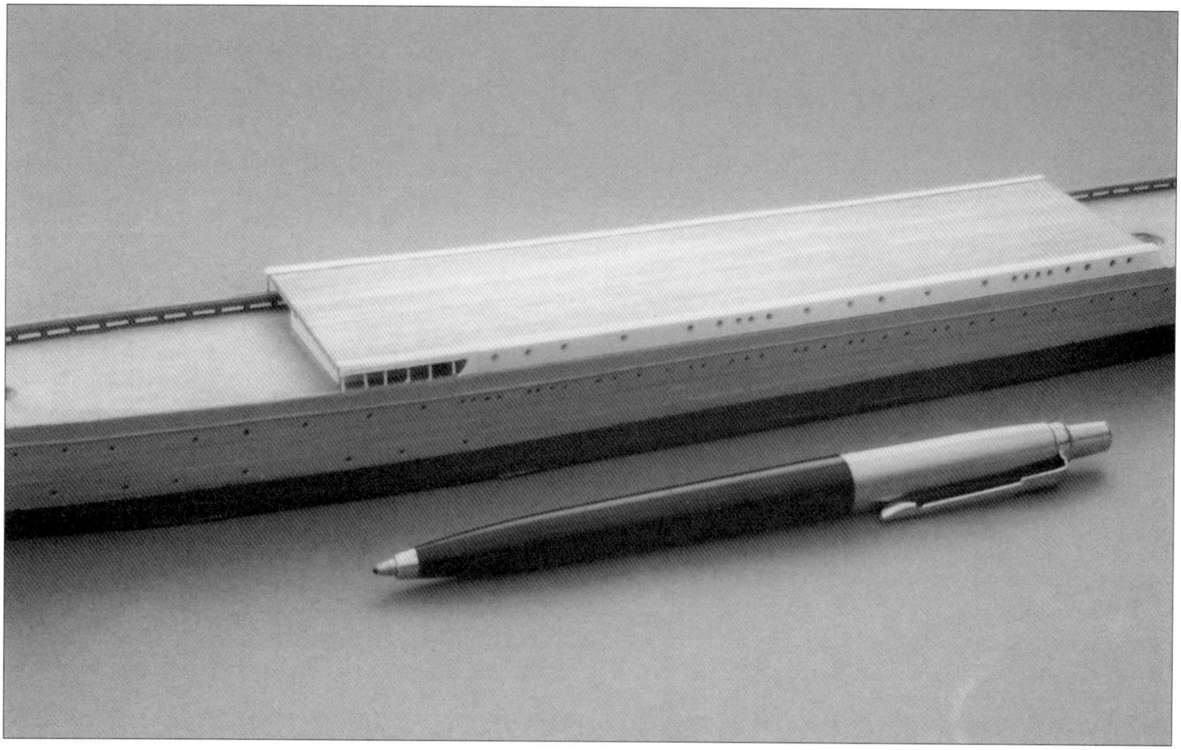

The hull has been plated, portholes drilled, and painted.

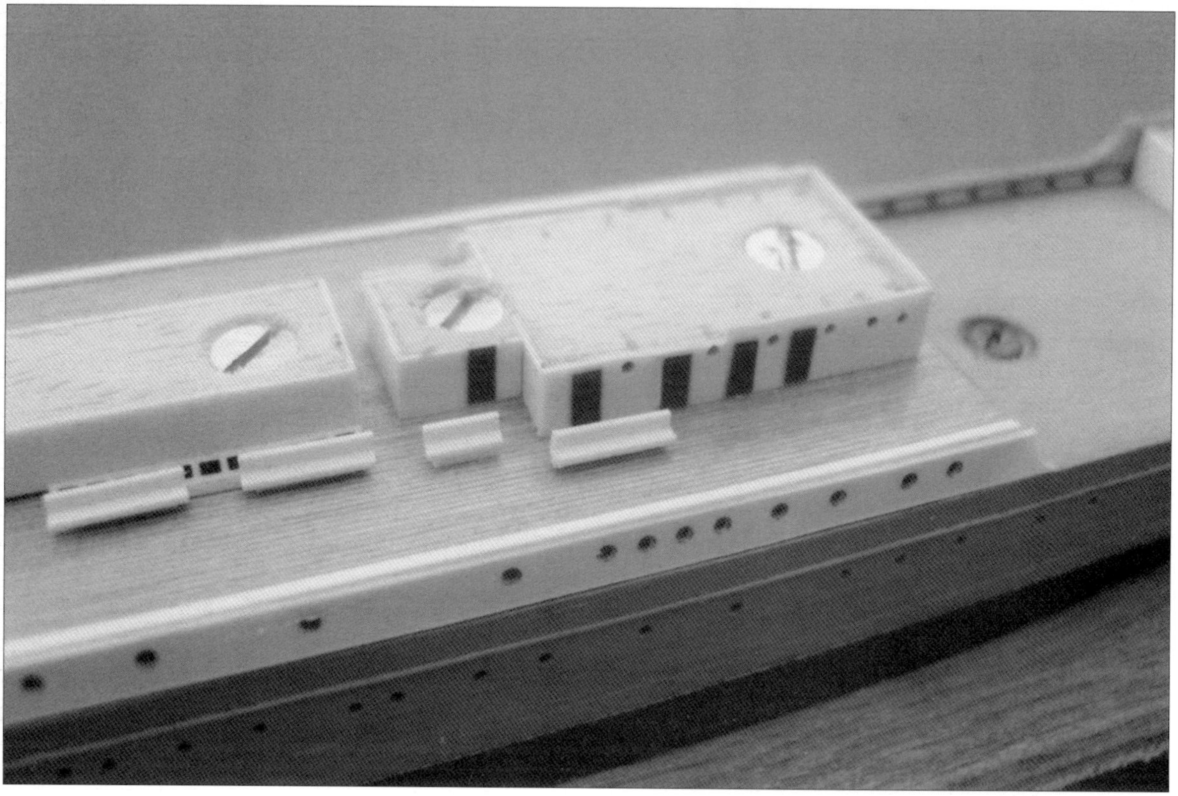

The forward end of the bridge deck. The two countersunk holes are for the bolts to secure the model to the baseboard.

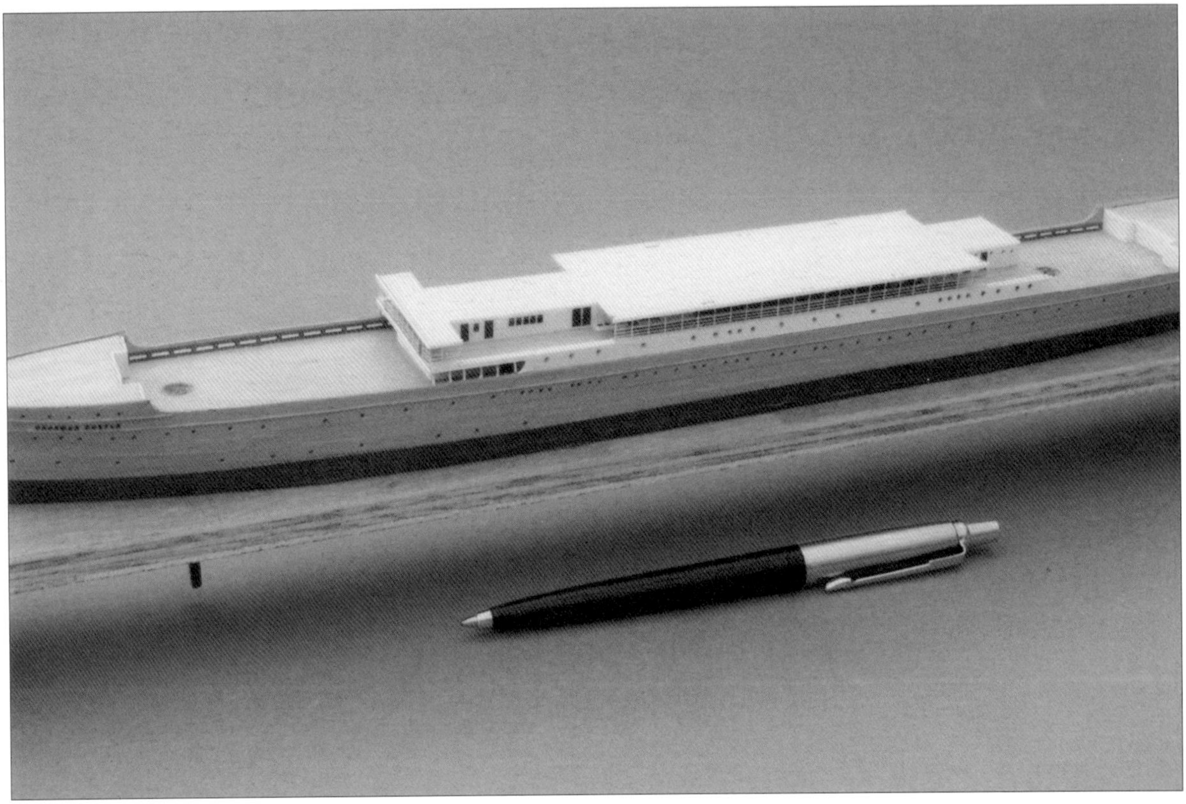

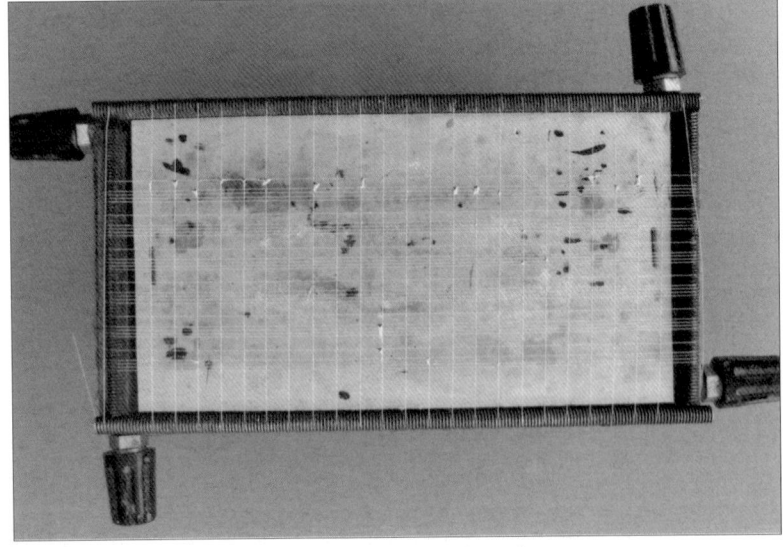

The boat deck with side stanchions and rails fitted.

During the Dardanelle's Campaign, the ship was used as a base hospital. As soon as she was filled to capacity with patients, they were taken to Italy. This service was marred by an incident in 1916 when she struck a mine in the Aegean Sea and had to be beached on the Greek island of Tinos. Several patients were killed in this incident. The ship was then towed to Malta where she lay in a damaged state for several months before being towed to La Spezia for a permanent repair.

When the War came to a close the twenty-year-old ship was sent to Murmansk for use as a base hospital during the Russian Revolution. The weather was bitterly cold and the open-sided decks were boarded up and her new appearance brought the nickname 'Noah's Ark' into common use. In 1919, the ship arrived in the UK carrying sick and injured patients, after which time she was handed back to the Union-Castle Line. The return to commercial employment was short-lived, however, and after only one voyage, she was once again acquired by the British Government, returning to Archangel, Russia, in 1921 to take out wounded and sick personnel and also non-Russian medical staff.

The rail frame, with rails and stanchions wound on and the initial soldering completed.

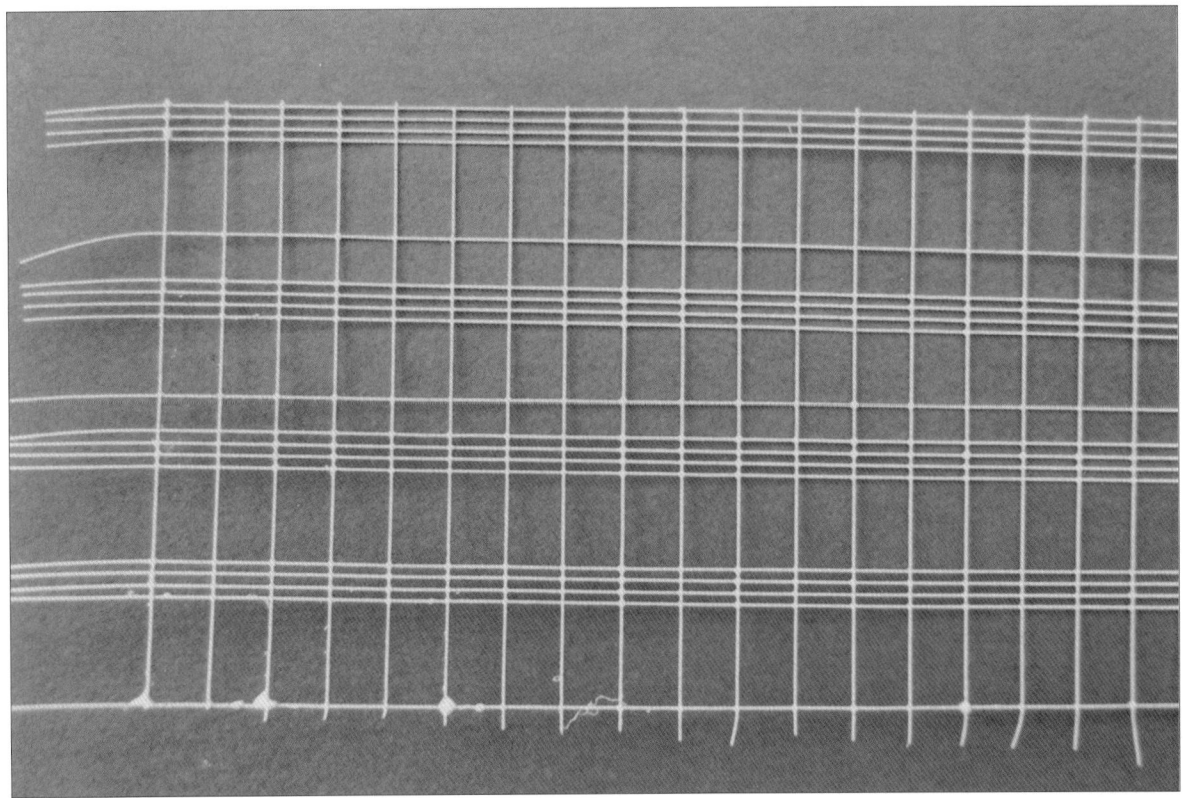

The rails soldered and painted.

When the port was finally evacuated, the *Braemar Castle* was the last to leave.

During the years spent as a hospital ship the *Braemar Castle* had carried just over 2,655,000 patients – a truly remarkable number! The final two years were spent as a troopship for the British peacekeeping force during the Turkish-Greek fighting. Late in the year 1924, the 26-year-old *Braemar Castle*, worn out by years of arduous service, was sold for £17,500 and went to Italy to be scrapped.

The model

I obtained the plans a number of years ago from either the National Maritime Museum, Greenwich, or the Mitchell Library, Glasgow, I cannot remember which one.

I decided to build the model to a scale of 1in = 32ft (1:384). This gave the model a hull length of about 14.5in overall.

The initial work did not take all that long. The cutting of the wood was expedited by the use of a small bandsaw. Most of the first hour was taken up scoring the ½2in marine plywood for the well decks forward and aft. I use marine plywood because it is not perfectly white and becomes darker when varnished. Years ago, I used a white chestnut veneer for the deck, but although this looked beautifully white, I felt that it was not accurate and prefer the darker looking wood. I noticed, too, long ago that the wooden decks of Union-Castle vessels changed colour depending on weather conditions. If it was raining and overcast in the Bay of Biscay, the decks would appear a dark brown, but in the tropics they would look almost white when dry and a bit darker during tropical rain. A number of people have said that the darker decks of merchant vessels were because they were not holystoned

regularly as they would be in naval ships. That is entirely a myth as far as the Union-Castle vessels were concerned. The decks of the six Union-Castle passenger ships in which I sailed were holystoned at about 0500 every morning with huge traditional holystones known as 'bibles' on the end of long wooden poles.

In the basic hull, the midship island is in three parts, a centre section and two outer sections. The outer sections are set in slightly from the sides to accommodate the solid bulwarks that run from forecastle to poop deck. By fitting the bulwarks in a single piece each side (glued to the sides of the raised midship island) adds strength and continuity.

The hull was plated with paper masking tape. The portholes were drilled into this before painting. The raised moulding around the hull at deck level was made from a piece of thin brass wire that had been stretched slightly to make it perfectly straight. It was secured in place with contact adhesive before the hull was painted.

The white upper part of the midship section was made from thin plasticard. The portholes were drilled in the plasticard sheet along a steel ruler used as a guide before it was cut down to size. I have found that drilling along a steel ruler is very good for keeping the portholes in line, but it can cause slight damage to the edge of the ruler. Because of this, I use an old ruler for this purpose. The drilled white strip fits snugly along the sides of the midship island above the full-length bulwarks. By fitting the white strip after painting the hull, a sharp junction between white and lavender hull colour was ensured.

The lavender hull paint was mixed from three small sample pots of fast drying enamel paint. I began with a half pot of smoke grey and added a small quantity of lavender,

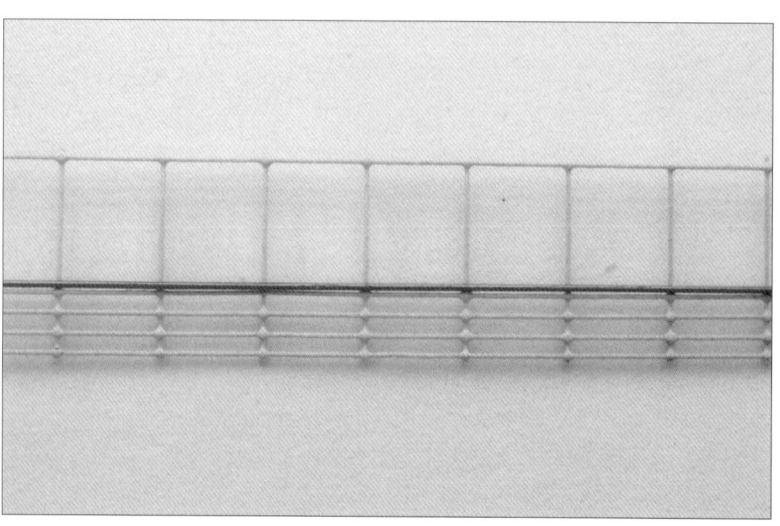

The rails with the simulated wood capping rail fitted.

followed by a small amount of harbour blue until I arrived at what I felt was the correct colour. Union-Castle hull colour can be rather difficult to achieve unless familiar with it. Fortunately, colour photographs of the ships are available on the internet or ship photograph agencies. What is correct or incorrect is still open to debate because the ships appeared to change colour depending on the weather conditions. On a winter day in Southampton they appeared plain grey, but on a sunny

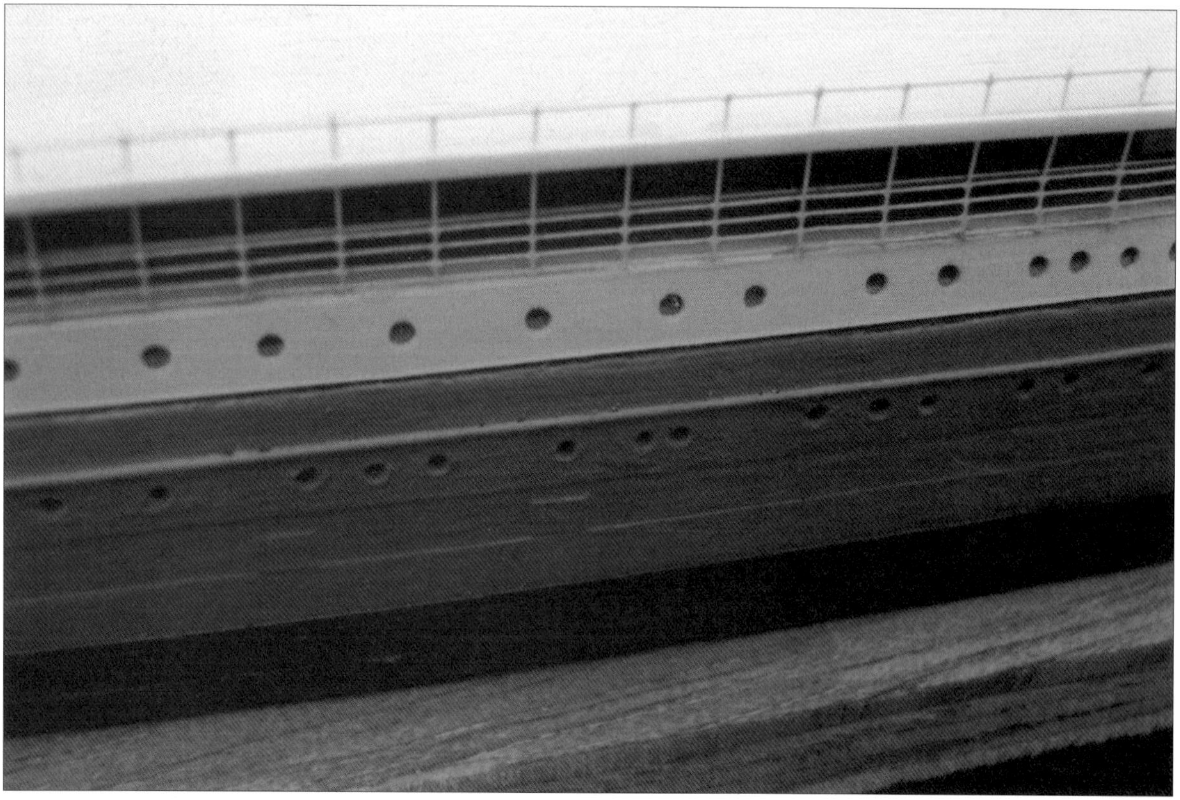

Rails fitted, and the thin strip of plasticard covering has been fitted to the edge of the boat deck.

Construction of the funnel.

day in the tropics or the South African ports, they appeared as they were meant to – a beautiful shade of lavender. The panels on the inside of the bulwarks of the well decks forward and aft were made on the computer, using the 'boxes, lines and squares' facility, which may be found in 'fonts' in the Microsoft Word word processing programme.

Where the top of the midship deck overhangs the forward end of the accommodation underneath, the side stanchions were made from small staples from a paper stapler cut off to an L-shape, painted, and glued in position, with the top part of the L glued to the underside of the deck above.

The two holes visible in the well decks are fixing holes. A long countersunk-head bolt was fitted in each one. These had to be of sufficient length to pass through the hull, the sea and also the baseboard. When the hull was finally fitted in the sea, a washer and nut were placed on the bottom of each bolt. The hole in the baseboard had also to be countersunk to accommodate washers and nuts. These two bolts were eventually covered with hatches, thus hiding them from view. It was important when countersinking these holes to ensure that the head of the bolt was just below the surface of the deck.

The top of the midship island is designated bridge deck, although the bridge itself is above this at the forward end of the boat deck. I made the public rooms and engine casing on this deck from wood faced with white plasticard. The portholes were drilled in these facing pieces before they were fitted. The long white seats were cut from L-shaped white plasticard angle strip. After the various parts of the casing and public rooms were glued on, I drilled holes through them and added fairly large

A cargo winch and the windlass.

countersunk screws to back up the glue. When positioning the screws, it was important to make sure that they did not lie below the position of the funnel or the large cowl ventilators that would require fixing holes. When the fittings on the bridge deck were completed, I fitted the scored boat deck on top.

The next task was to make and fit the rails and side stanchions between the bridge deck and the boat deck. On previous models of similar ships, I had etched these out of thin brass shim. Although it was successful and very neat, there are several disadvantages to etching. A quantity of brass shim has to be obtained and it can be hard to find and quite expensive. Preparing the brass by masking off the stanchions is quite time consuming. The etching itself is slow and uses fairly hazardous etching chemicals, requiring a great deal of care and safety precautions. Finally, I

have found that I do not always achieve a perfect set of etchings first time and have to go through the whole laborious process again. With the *Braemar Castle*, I decided to solder the whole lot with the stanchions between the decks simply being extensions of the vertical rail stanchions. As usual, I wound the rails and stanchions on a rail frame, a simple board edged with threaded rod and four old radio terminal set in the sides to use as anchoring for the start and end of the winding. For this I use 38swg tinned copper wire because it is easy to handle and looks correct even though it is slightly over scale. The horizontal bars were wound on first. Each length of rail consisted of four horizontals, a space and then a single supporting horizontal. This will be removed later. The soldering of the rails is easier than it sounds. The whole framework was painted with a liquid sol-

dering flux and the soldering iron, with a fair amount of solder on it, was run lightly up each vertical, ignoring any extra blobs of solder that inevitably form. These may be seen in the illustration. This first solder run is to make most of the joints and give the whole winding some support. I then gave it a second coat of flux and again ran the iron, this time without much solder on it, up the verticals. This was repeated until all the excess blobs had disappeared and all the crossovers had been soldered. The set of rails was then cut from the frame and washed in water to remove excess flux. Holding the rails at the edge with a pair of surgical clamps, I sprayed the rails lightly with white matt primer. This produced a very neat set of rails all ready for use.

A single strip of rails, complete with the horizontal support rail was then cut from the assembly. A piece

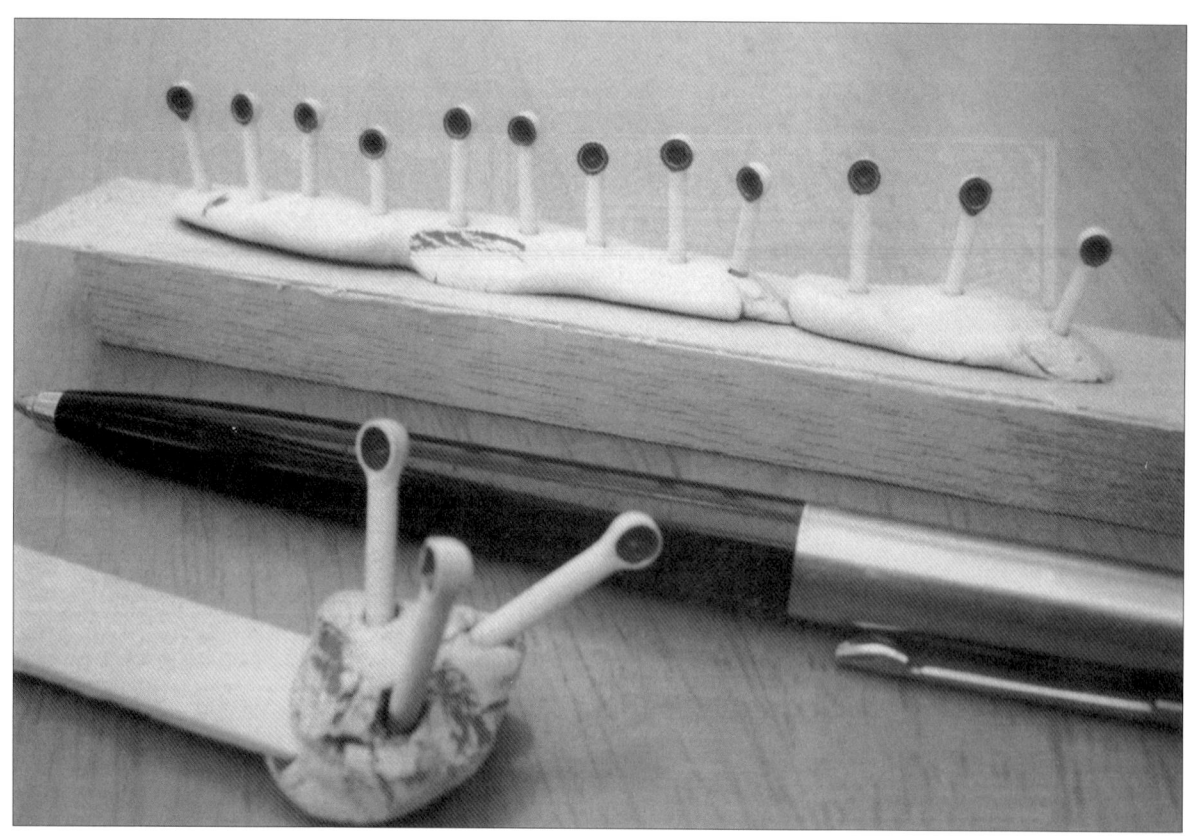

Cowl ventilators held on a piece of Plasticine for painting.

With the funnel fitted the model is beginning to take shape.

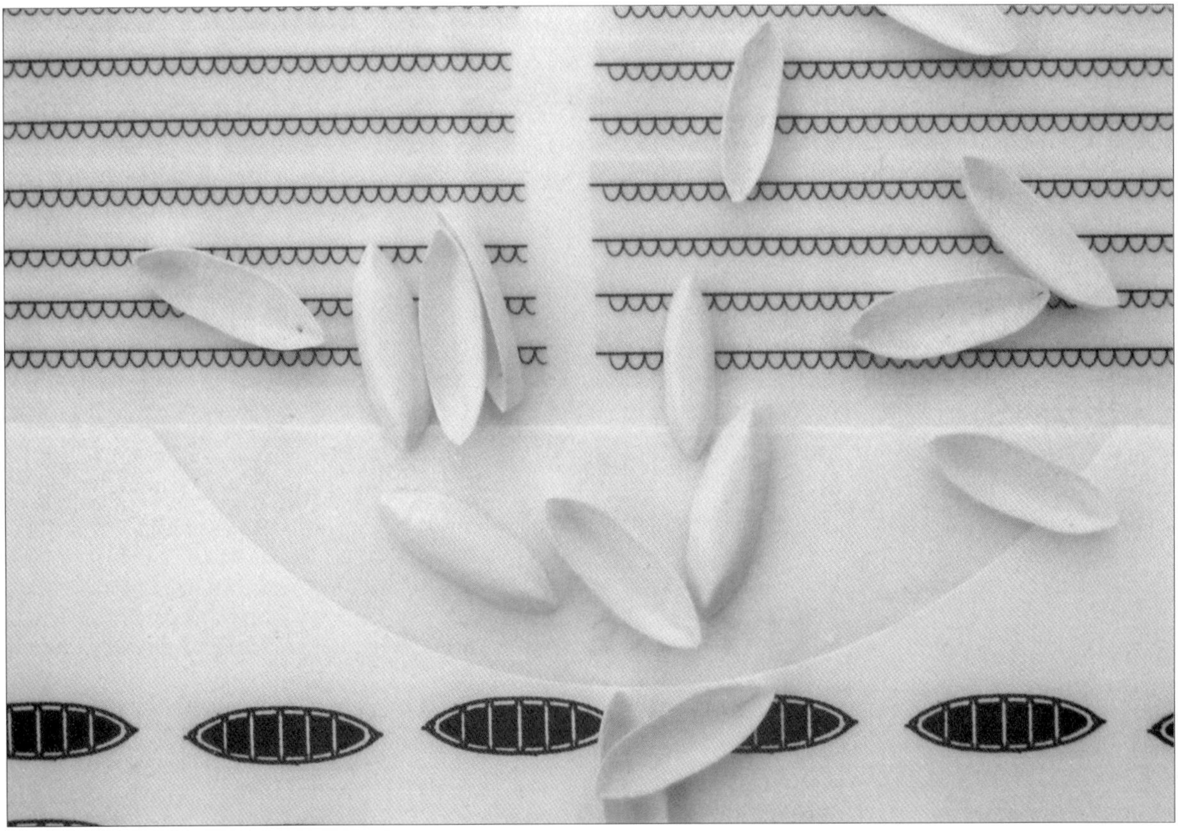

The vacuum formed boats during construction.

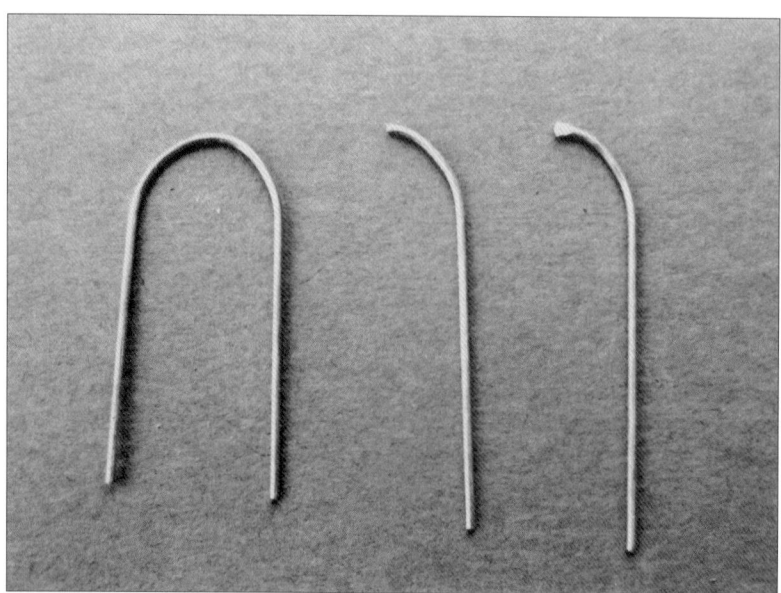

Construction of radial type davits. Bend wire to U-shape. Cut at top and to length to form two davits. Squeeze top end to form simulated ring eye to take the falls.

of brown enamelled copper wire was stretched slightly, cut to length and glued along the top horizontal to represent the wood capping rail. The piece of rail was then glued to the model using contact adhesive. At this stage, the vertical stanchions, together with their temporary support, still project above the boat deck. The lower bar of the rails rests on top of the white upper side plat-ing of the hull, whilst the vertical stanchions are glued to the edge of the boat deck. These are then covered with a thin strip of white plasti-card.

When the rails are in position and the thin strip of plasticard is glued along the edge of the boat deck over the top end of the stan-chions, the tops of the stanchions and the support wire may be trimmed off. This may be accom-plished very quickly and easily with a pair of micro shears. This small, but useful, tool is commonly used by electronic engineers to snip small components from printed circuit boards. In the UK, they may be obtained from Maplin Electronics.

As the funnel was perfectly round in cross section, it was simply cut from a length of tube of the right diameter using a small pipe cutter. Four rings were lightly scored into the tube also using the pipe cutter. As well as representing the plating joins, the top one was also useful when painting the black top section. A base plate with a central fixing hole was soldered on the bottom and then trimmed off with tin snips and a smooth file. The bottom of the funnel had, of course, been filed off to the angle of rake before the base-plate was added.

The parts of the winches and windlass were turned from small pieces of brass rod and assembled and secured on thin plywood bases, before being spray-painted satin black. The windlass was not a con-ventional type, but appeared to be a combination of steam drive and manual drive via the capstan.

Each of the large cowl ventilators was made in two parts, the shaft and the cowl. The cowls were turned from brass rod and hollowed out after shaping. The rod was placed in the lathe chuck and the end rounded off with a smooth file held on it as the chuck rotated. The cowl was then parted off using a jeweller's saw. The solid cowl was then placed into the lathe chuck, rounded end first. A dental burr with a ball end was placed in the tail chuck and advanced into the cowl to hollow it out. Finally, the cowl was soldered to the trunk and the ventilator spray-painted white, with the inside of the cowl hand-painted red.

The fifteen lifeboats were vacuum formed using the methods described in *MS129*. That issue also contains plans and constructional details on

Making the engine room skylight from thin plasticard.

Port bow view of the completed model.

Finished model seen from the starboard quarter.

Braemar Castle model in its showcase.

Photographs by the author.

making a miniature vacuum box for use in combination with a normal domestic vacuum cleaner. The boat grab lines and the thwarts were made on the computer. This method of making small boats works well on miniatures, but would probably not be as effective on larger models. The davits were of the radial type and simple to produce. A piece of 24swg tinned copper wire was stretched slightly to make it straight. It was then bent over a round rod and cut in two at the top using a scalpel. Finally, the top was pinched with a pair of mole grips to represent the ringbolt for the falls. On a miniature model there is no need to drill the hole in the simulated ringbolt as the falls will just be glued direct to the pinched end at the top of the davit.

The skylight panels were made on the computer and printed on to a self-adhesive sheet. This was then stuck on a sheet of thin plasticard,

cut out and scored down the centre. The plasticard was cracked along the score and glued to another thin piece of card with a suitable plastic weld. In the case of the engine-room skylights, two scores were required as it had a flat top section. The black sections of the skylight were capital letter I from the Arial Black font, printed in bold to the required size. Once the plastic weld had set, each open end of the skylight was placed on a thin sheet of plasticard and more plastic weld applied. After it had dried, the surplus plasticard was trimmed off with a scalpel, thus closing up the ends.

The masts were just long tapered spars. They were made from brass rod filed into a taper and placed in a 12-volt hand-held electric drill for the final smoothing with various grades of carborundum paper. I used only 6 volts on the drill. The full voltage would make the brass whip

round and maybe even fly out of the drill. It is essential to use protective goggles when doing this kind of work. The large gaff sails were made from white airmail paper on which I had printed grey lines using the computer. I use grey rather than black so they are not so obtrusive. The sails were moulded around an ostrich egg whilst wet in order to get the wind-filled shape. I covered both the tapering of spars and the sail-making in more detail in *MS128* (four-masted barque *Jacqueline*).

The rigging was done with fine copper wire. The methods used have been described in my previous articles *MS128, 130, 131, 134, 135, 138* and *139*.

By the time the model was complete, the painted Plasticine sea was ready. The model was set in the sea, and then secured in its glass case. An article devoted to 'Making and Painting Seas' appeared in *MS137*.❑

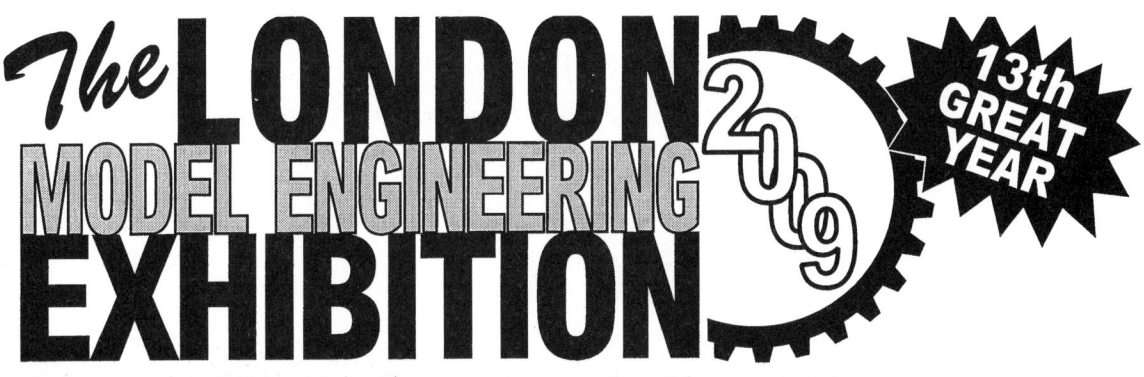

The LONDON MODEL ENGINEERING EXHIBITION 2009

13th GREAT YEAR

16th, 17th & 18th JANUARY 2009
ALEXANDRA PALACE

The South's Model Engineering & Modelling Exhibition!

WORKING MODELS

FREE CAR PARKING

Locomotives, Traction and Stationary Engines, Workshop Tools, etc.
– *PLUS* –
ALL THE LEADING SPECIALIST SUPPLIERS

MARINE MODELLING
See all types of boats from the man of war to modern tugs, yachts, etc.

LIVE STEAM
Locomotives and HOT AIR ENGINES IN ACTION

MODEL ENGINEERING

Superb displays by leading model engineering clubs & societies

OPEN: 10.00am until 5.30pm Friday & Saturday, 10.00am until 4.00pm Sunday
(Last Admissions one hour before closing)

Admission: Adult £9.50, Senior £8.50, Child £5.50, Family 1 (1 adult + 3 children) £15, Family 2 (2 adults + 3 children) £24.50

Organised by Meridienne Exhibitions Ltd, The Fosse, Fosse Way, Leamington Spa, Warks. CV31 1XN

Tel: 01926 614101   Fax: 01926 614293   E-mail: info@meridienneexhibitions.co.uk   Web: www.londonmodelengineering.co.uk

MODELLER'S
Draught

Orkney Pilot Boat
Scapa Pilot

by J Pottinger

T his vessel, the *Scapa Pilot*, was one of the popular Talis-man designs by the Murray Cormack Associates, Naval Architects, and was one of several completed as pilot boats.

The concept was that these vessels combined relatively high speeds with seaworthiness to carry out pilotage duties in often exposed locations around the coast.

The Murray Cormack Associates partnership was established in 1972 by Maitland Murray and the late Douglas Cormack, later to be joined by Dennis Davidson and Jim Abernethy. They all have extensive experience afloat, backed by periods spent with well-known naval architect and shipbuilding companies.

Murray Cormack Associates designed the highly successful 15m round bilge semi-displacement Talisman 49 hull form in 1974. The first of many commercial versions of the GRP Talisman 49 was completed in 1975 as the 20-knot twin-screw pilot launch with what became a standard Talisman arrangement, engines aft and gearboxes forward in a U-drive configuration, allowing easy removal of the engines via the clear after deck, and keeping the noise away from the wheelhouse and forward accommodation. As well as commercial pilot and patrol launches a number of yachts have used this hull design.

Derived from the Talisman 49 were the North 40/45 and 58/65 versions built in GRP, aluminium alloy and steel.

Three of the 20m North 65 class operate in the most exposed waters found in the UK at Sullom Voe oil terminal in Shetland. Two vessels of the same hull form replaced the subject of these plans for duty in the

1. Alongside view, showing toe-rail slightly raised as approaching the bow which has a prominent bull's-eye.

2. This shows the after end of the deckhouse, with wheelhouse entrance to starboard. The navigation sidelights are set on raised mountings on each side of the wheelhouse top. Note the guardrails are carried aft around the ends of the wheelhouse sides and on the central trunking. The large vent inlet grille can be seen.

Orkney Pilotage service in the Pentland Firth. The vessel was put up for sale in 2005.

Specification

Built: 1976.
Length overall: 48.25ft.
Beam: 14.5ft.
Draught, maximum: 5.5ft.
Gross tonnage: 32.5 tons.
Machinery: Two Volvo Penta diesels 246.2kw.
Speed: 18knots.

3. The wheelhouse front with hatch and lifebuoy stowage. Note the safety harness rail, the grab rail, and the glazed hatch.

4. Quarter forward view showing the various radar scanners and searchlight. Note the MOB davits which have been omitted from the plans. This view shows the recessed deck lights in the sides of the deckhouse.

5. Top of wheelhouse showing various fittings, including loud hailer, searchlights and radar scanner.

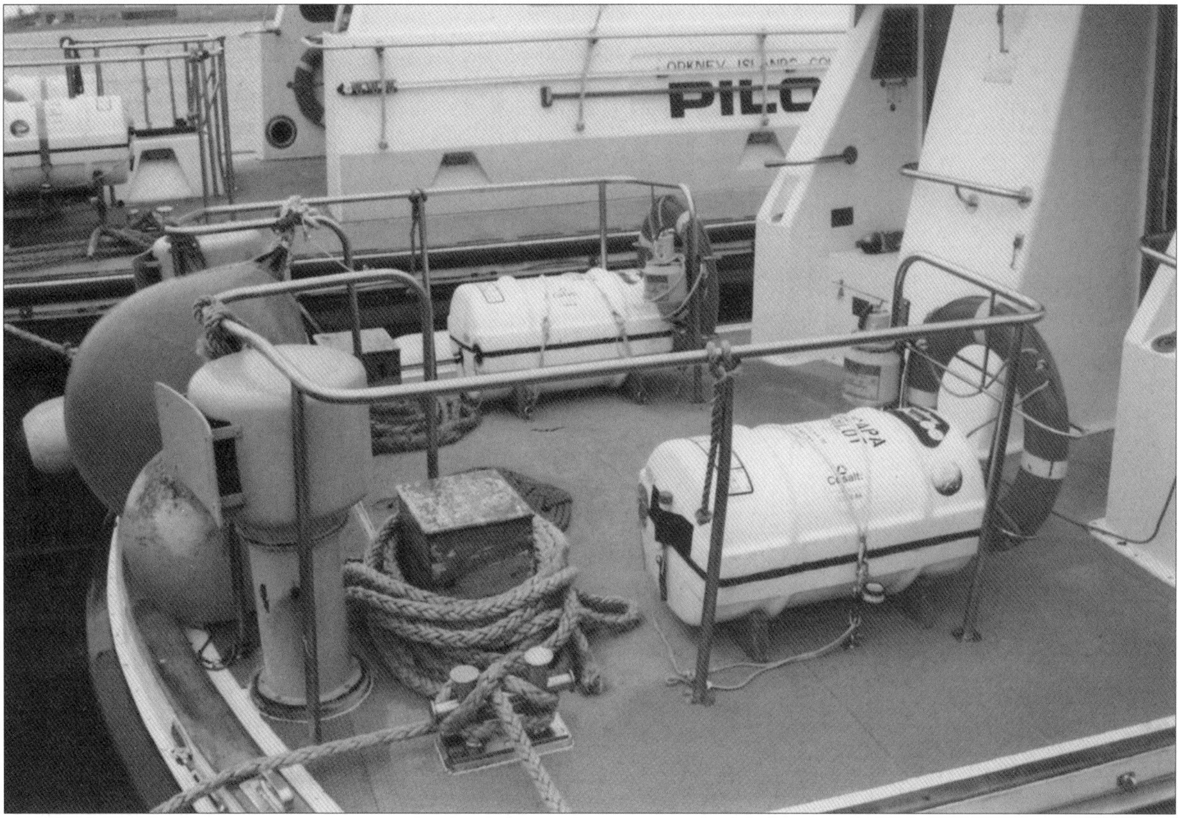

6. After deck showing liferaft stowage and one of the engine room mushroom vents. This also shows the central trunk supporting the mast. The varnished wooden 'boxes' are covered up emergency pumps.

Examination of the lines and body plan will show a very easily driven hull on a light displacement, with a very much rounded bottom, and having a distinct lack of hard and flattish bilge. It would appear that she would roll in a seaway, but as a tried and tested design it is obviously no detriment to performance.

It will be noted that there is a sharp change of section and step at the line of chine. For model purposes it may be preferable to plank the hull all over as normal and then add another thickness to the upper hull above the chine line in order to represent the change of section.

A narrow knuckle extends all the way around the hull to form a base for the rubbing strake. Above this the sides are sloped inboard, being the outboard edge of the slightly raised moulded toe-rail. A section through this can be seen in detail on sketch A–A on Sheet 1.

The deckhouse has a fairly complicated shape, and will need to be well studied in order to construct it satisfactorily. It does, however, have

7. Nameboard and liferaft stowage on top of the wheelhouse. The port navigation sidelight is mounted on the tall side board.

8. Detail of mast and the various navigation lights. The mast lights are all white except the two positioned at the lower level on the fore and aft side of the mast, which are red.

the advantage that it can be made to lift off as a whole unit to give access to the inside of the hull.

There are two glazed hatches on top of the forward part of the deck-house, and another on the fore deck. The cowl ventilators are mounted on top of spray boxes as can be seen in Photographs 1 and 4.

I have omitted the Man Overboard Davits seen in the photographs for reasons of simplicity. It will be noted that the guardrails are attached to the deckhouse, as is common on pilot boats, instead of being at the deck edge. The safety harness rail is fitted slightly lower down. The deck lights are fitted in recesses in the sides of the deckhouse.

A better appreciation of much of the detail, and colour scheme, can be obtained from study of the photographs.

Colour scheme

Black: hull. Orkney Islands Council logo on deckhouse, ship's name on varnished backboard.

+*White:* deckhouse, wheelhouse, liferaft canisters, numeral 1 on bow, toe-rail.

Buff: mast, various radar supports and loudhailer support, mushroom vents at stern.

Red/orange: lifebuoys.

Light brown: deck.

Varnished wood: top of toe-rail. ❑

9. Fore deck view which shows the toe rail with hardwood capping, also the vertical capstan, hatch, and mooring bollards. The rope lengths with knotted ends are for use by the crew and pilots when standing at the rail whilst approaching a vessel.

Photographs from the author's collection.

HMS *Roebuck*

by Bernard Baldwin

In the last quarter of the eighteenth century the Royal Navy found itself engaged in a conflict off the east coast of America where unpopular laws and heavy taxes imposed by the British Government had caused a rebellion by the local colonies. The colonialists were waging the war using relatively small, lightly armed ships capable of negotiating the shallow waters from Chesapeake Bay and up the eastern seaboard to New York and Long Island. It was quickly realised by the British this was not a situation requiring large ships of the line, more a case for fast, well-armed, handy ships which could harass the enemy among the shoals and shallows of the area. HMS *Roebuck* was ideally suited for just this type of work. Launched from Chatham Dockyard in April 1774 she was one of the first of a series of twenty-five similar ships, which would be built over the coming years. Armed with twenty 18pdr on the gun deck, twenty-two 9pdr on the upper deck and two 6 pdr on the forecastle, she was well equipped to cope with any adversary liable to be encountered in the area. Two rows of gun ports and two apparent tiers of windows across the stern and quarter galleries gave her the appearance, through the inadequate telescopes of the day, of a much larger ship. However, closer examination of the upper tier of windows and galleries would reveal there were no cabins behind them, their lower levels coinciding with the level of the quarterdeck; they were indeed quite false and probably intended to deceive any intending aggressor.

In the September of 1775 *Roebuck* sailed in the company of other ships to assist the North Atlantic Squadron in suppressing the rebellion, and there she stayed for the first six years of her career. That career would include cruises in the North

Port side view of finished model.

The quarterdeck.

The forecastle with its two 6pdr, the belayed ropes and the galley chimney, behind the shrouds.

Sea, the Channel, and around the Windward Islands, service as a troop carrier and a hospital ship before ending in her final paying off in the July of 1811.

It is fortunate the draught of the ship is held at the National Maritime Museum, Greenwich, London, along with, unusually, details of the ship's carvings (see *MS100*). The eminent American ship modeller Harold Hahn used this information to produce a set of drawings to a scale of ⅛in = 1ft (1:96), ideally suited to the production of a model. I obtained a copy of these and reduced them, where necessary, to ¹⁄₁₆in = 1ft, (1:192) scale. My previous models had all been built to a scale of 1in = 50ft (1:600) so this was a new venture for me, demanding new skills. The model, which is built in the style of a Dockyard Model but with fully rigged masts and spars, has a hull of pear wood. This was produced by gluing together ¹⁄₁₆in thick wafers of the wood to form a block, wide enough to accommodate the beam and about ¾in (18mm) deeper than the greatest distance from the keel to the highest timberhead in the hull. The wafers are grouped into pairs, a central slot, which would eventually house the keel, being cut in one edge to assist location during assembly. A flat base was prepared with each hull station clearly marked upon it and a firm stop at station No. 1, at the bow. Two wooden battens ⅛in x 1¼in (3mm x 32mm) were screwed to the base, parallel to and equidistant from the centreline, with sufficient distance apart to just accommodate the width of the wafer. These and the surface of the base were then well rubbed with candle wax to prevent any glue adhering to them. A length of wood longer than the hull and a push fit into the keel slot was used to act as a false keel during assembly. The first pair of wafers was assembled together using two or three spots of PVA glue, slotted on to the false keel and located against the stop, with the keel uppermost, and precisely over the hull centre line. It was important the keel piece remained precisely over the centreline during the whole assembly of the block, otherwise a misaligned hull would be produced. At no time was it allowed to become glued to the wafers. Before each pair was glued into the block it was clearly marked with a number in the centre of its face indicating its correct position along the hull, e.g. 21, 21A etc.

The nominal ¹⁄₁₆in thick wafers were in fact produced in three different thicknesses, nominal, 10 per cent 0.004in (0.1mm) thicker, and 10 per cent or 0,004in thinner than nominal. This was to allow for the correction of cumulative errors during assembly. If the wafer pairs began to

Amidships showing the ship's boats, Note the capstan beneath.

fall behind or move ahead of their station, thicker or thinner wafers would be used successively to recover the situation. During this phase, longitudinal clamps were used to pull the wafers tightly together and great care taken to ensure they remained perpendicular to the centreline and the keel piece exactly over the centre. With all fifty-eight perpendicular wafers pairs in place and the glue dry, the block was secured to the base by two wood-screws and the stop removed. Wafers for the cant frames could now be fitted. These were the same basic wafer pairs but split vertically along the centre line and tapered from the outside to the centre. They are used at the bow and stern where the hull curves sharply into the stem and sternpost, and reduce the amount of bevelling that would occur on the outer edge of a perpendicular frame. Figure 1 shows the general arrangement. With the glue thoroughly dry, the side battens could be removed and with the base plate acting as a

reference plane, the block was carved to shape using chisels, sandpaper and the normal card templates. The finished hull block was then sandpapered to the surface finish that would be required on the completed model. No further sandpapering would be possible after the frames had been reassembled. The rising floor line at bow and stern, the lower and upper lines of the main wale, the line of the frame heads and the cut off line were all pencilled on to the block using card templates. The cut off line is the point at which all the frames would eventually be cut through in order to remove the partially finished hull from the base. The two battens used previously were shaped to fit tightly around the hull block at its junction with the base, before being secured to the base plate. These would form the location points during the reassembly, so it was important they were in contact with every wafer. After removal from the base plate, the block was dismantled by progres-

sively immersing one end in cellulose thinners until the adhesive was loosened and the wafer could be removed. This operation was carried out in the open air for health and safety reasons. As each wafer pair was taken off, the legibility of the station numbers was checked, before it was laid out, in sequence, on a flat board to dry.

After two days all traces of the thinners had evaporated. Adhesive was applied to the areas indicated in Figure 2, and using the keel slot and the location points to align them correctly, the wafers were joined together again into pairs. To transform these into frames that would ultimately form the hull it was necessary to remove material from the centre. The depth of each frame varies as it progresses from the frame head, where it is the same in depth as in thickness, i.e. square, to a maximum at the keel slot. A line, to indicate this variation and define that part of the wafer to be removed, was drawn in. Material was removed

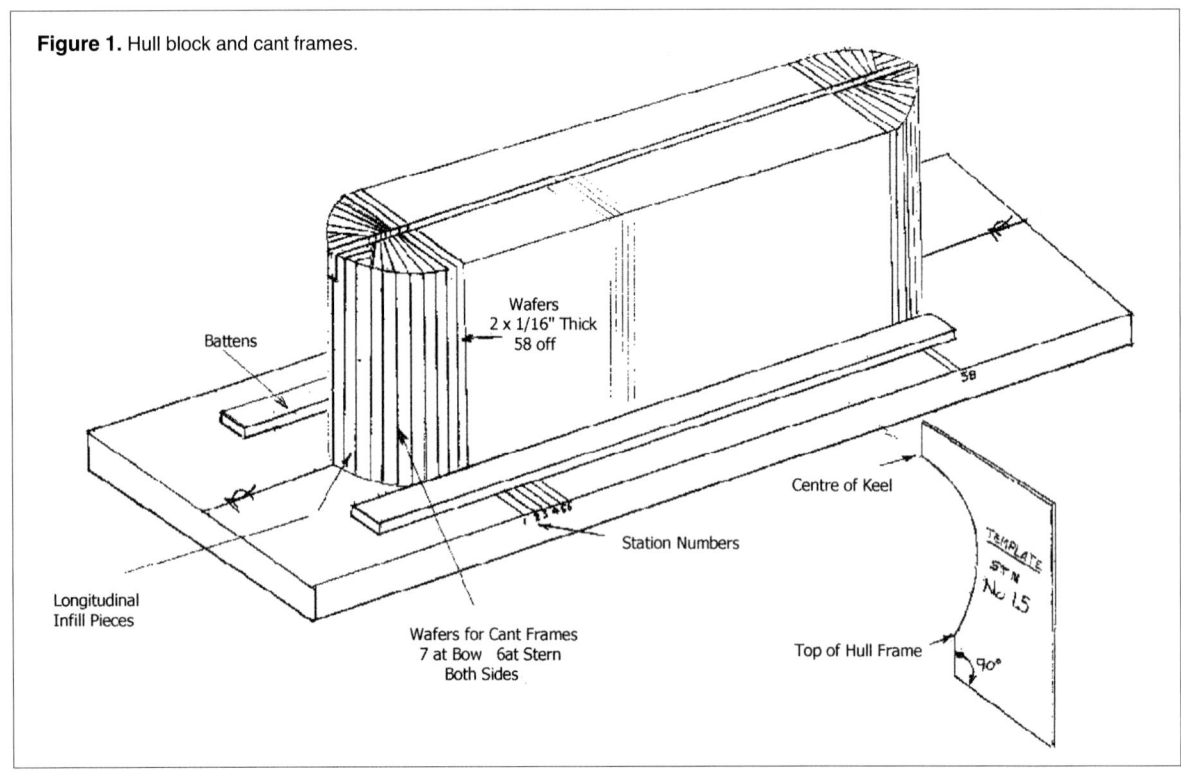

Figure 1. Hull block and cant frames.

The fore chains.

Figure 2. Frame reassembly.

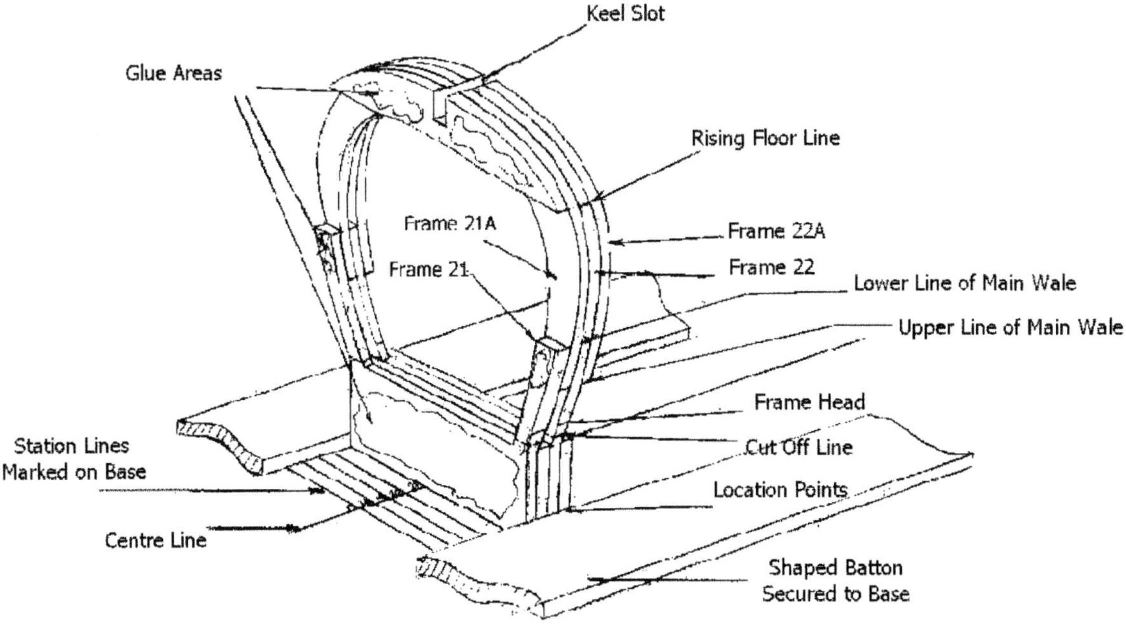

Keel Slot

Glue Areas

Rising Floor Line

Frame 21A

Frame 22A

Frame 21

Frame 22

Lower Line of Main Wale

Upper Line of Main Wale

Frame Head

Station Lines
Marked on Base

Cut Off Line

Location Points

Centre Line

Shaped Batton
Secured to Base

The rising floor line at the bow.

The port bow and anchor. Note the clinker-built launch.

The rising floor line at the stern.

The port quarter gallery.

using chain drilling, dental burrs and a scalpel, with an area approximately ½in above the location points and the full distance between them left in place to stabilise each assembly and to provide an area for the frame identification number to be rewritten. To generate the gaps between the futtocks it was necessary to remove a different portion of each frame pair. On frame 21 clean cuts were made at the rising floor line and at the lower line of the main wale and the portion between them removed, there being no adhesive at this point they came away cleanly. Similarly, on frame 21A, a portion between the upper main wale line and a point ⅛in (3mm) above the cut off line was removed. With all the wafers similarly treated and converted into frames, the final assembly could commence. Frames 21 and 21A were fitted back on to the base exactly on the correct station line, this time being glued at the location points and adjusted carefully to ensure they were perpendicular to the centre line in both horizontal and vertical planes. When the glue was dry, frames 22 and 22A could be fitted using the keel slot and location points to ensure correct alignment. With all the fifty-eight perpendicular frames fixed in place, the keel, stem and sternpost were added before fitting the cant frames.

Construction continued with the fitting of the main wale, cut from African Blackwood, the gun wale from Cherry wood and ancillary planking from Castello Box. Transom pieces were fitted, greatly stabilising the stern frames, before the gun ports were cut and framed. The whole structure was now stable, and although still quite delicate, it was possible to sever the frames at the cut-off lines and remove the hull from its base. The assembly could now be fixed to temporary cradles and a few deck beams fitted at the upper deck level to prevent damage during work on the orlop and the gun decks.

The foregoing is intended to be a simplified account of the construction of the hull, other problems were encountered en-route, all proved interesting and satisfying to overcome; but is not that part of the pleasure of scratch building? However, it is not a project I would recommend to an inexperienced modeller. Methods that are more conventional were used for the rest of the model. Decks were laid, using holly planks 0.030in (0.75mm) wide x 0.010in (0.25mm) thick, over car-

The figurehead.

The stern carvings.

lings and deck beams of pear wood. The figurehead, a female figure wielding a spear, was carved from boxwood whilst the spear shaft was made from copper wire. Ranged across the stern are a number of carved figures; the head and shoulders of a female, a dog, a deer with antlers, four angels and a spear-wielding hunter on each quarter. Too small to carve individually, their outlines were cut from boxwood, glued on to a false stern board of African Blackwood before being carved to shape using dental burrs and miniature chisels. The use of a false stern board allowed the carving tools to cut into the board and a little behind the figures, giving a better impression of relief. After gilding, they were floated off the false board using methylated spirits to soften the PVA adhesive, and then glued into posi-

The main and mizzen fighting tops.

tion on the model. Guns were turned from African Blackwood, which I find a reasonable substitute for Ebony and somewhat less expensive. Those on the gun deck, although unseen in the finished model, are mounted on carriages, complete with tackle, not as silly as it may sound, as they were used to practise the technique before making those on the upper deck, which can be seen. A 29ft pinnace and a 30ft launch were clinker built around a carved wooden plug over which cling film was stretched to prevent the glue sticking to it. The launch has a gun mounting in the bow and the pinnace is decorated around the stern as was the custom of the day. Masts and spars were turned from Castello Box, a wood similar to lemonwood that has a nice buff colour and turns very well. Main and fore masts are finished and banded and all three stepped on the keel. Annealed Nickel/Chrome wire 0.006in dia. (0.15mm) was used for both standing and running rigging. The annealing was carried out by holding 12in (300mm) lengths between two pairs of pliers, and passing the wire through a candle flame whilst applying slight tension. The result is a length of wire, fairly straight, dull grey in colour and ready to be painted. It holds a catenary well, puts no tension on the masts, and is unaffected by humidity. A single strand served for running rigging, two strands twisted together for shrouds, and three strands twisted together for the main and fore stays and the anchor cable: hawser or cable laid cable as appropriate. Canadian Maple was used for the case, the glass being fitted into grooves in the frame pieces and the whole finished with matt polyurethane varnish.

The model took about 1,300 hours, spread over four years, to complete and was awarded the President's Cup and a gold medal at the Society of Model Shipwrights exhibition 2006, a gold medal and The Maze Challenge Cup at the Model Engineering Exhibition at Ascot in 2007.

References

Ships of the American Revolution and their Models by Harold H Hahn.
Eighteenth-Century Rigs and Rigging by Karl Heinz Marquardt.
Arming and Fitting of English Ships of War by Brian Lavery.
Construction and Fitting of the Sailing Man of War 1650-1850 by Peter Goodwin.
Masting and Rigging of English Ships of War 1625-1860 by James Lees.
Model Shipwright 100, article by Elizabeth Tucker.

The foremast and spars.

Photographs by the author.